MW00718071

About This Book

What can you achieve with this book?

This book is a guide for managers who are considering outsourcing all or some of the training function. It has stories and guidelines to help managers, whether they are from training, HRD, procurement, finance, or the line organization more fully understand what leads to a successful outsourcing relationship. It contains suggestions on when, what, to whom, and how to outsource specific training deliverables and the whole function.

Why is this topic important?

This book was written because of growing interest in outsourcing training. Organizations are spending millions of dollars annually on training and are looking for ways to reap better returns on that investment. Outsourcing is one solution because it can help organizations better manage their investment, leverage the technological capabilities of vendors, and avoid future liabilities associated with hiring training professionals. However, the solution is not without risks. It requires leadership to manage the relationship. It also requires ongoing oversight to assure the intellectual capital of the organization is protected and the developmental needs of employees are being met in the most cost-effective ways.

How is this book organized?

Every chapter contains stories, guidelines, and checklists you can use to:

- Determine if and how outsourcing would be of benefit to you.
- Clarify what type of external resources you would most benefit from.
- Determine what you can and should expect of external resources.
- Specify what you require in terms of program deliverables, reports, quality assurance, service level, risk management, and reporting relationships.
- Determine your level of readiness to outsource, ranging from managing the T&D function as a whole to coordinating specific process elements.
- Consider contractual elements that best protect your interests.
- Collaborate effectively with the functions involved in outsourcing decisions.

About Pfeiffer

Pfeiffer serves the professional development and hands-on resource needs of training and human resource practitioners and gives them products to do their jobs better. We deliver proven ideas and solutions from experts in HR development and HR management, and we offer effective and customizable tools to improve workplace performance. From novice to seasoned professional, Pfeiffer is the source you can trust to make yourself and your organization more successful.

Essential Knowledge Pfeiffer produces insightful, practical, and comprehensive materials on topics that matter the most to training and HR professionals. Our Essential Knowledge resources translate the expertise of seasoned professionals into practical, how-to guidance on critical workplace issues and problems. These resources are supported by case studies, worksheets, and job aids and are frequently supplemented with CD-ROMs, websites, and other means of making the content easier to read, understand, and use.

Essential Tools Pfeiffer's Essential Tools resources save time and expense by offering proven, ready-to-use materials—including exercises, activities, games, instruments, and assessments—for use during a training or team-learning event. These resources are frequently offered in looseleaf or CD-ROM format to facilitate copying and customization of the material.

Pfeiffer also recognizes the remarkable power of new technologies in expanding the reach and effectiveness of training. While e-hype has often created whizbang solutions in search of a problem, we are dedicated to bringing convenience and enhancements to proven training solutions. All our e-tools comply with rigorous functionality standards. The most appropriate technology wrapped around essential content yields the perfect solution for today's on-the-go trainers and human resource professionals.

Pfeiffer
www.pfeiffer.com

Essential resources for training and HR professionals

Outsourcing Training and Development

Factors for Success

Judith Hale

Pfeiffer
A Wiley Imprint
www.pfeiffer.com

Published by Pfeiffer
An Imprint of Wiley.
989 Market Street, San Francisco, CA 94103-1741 www.pfeiffer.com

ISBN: 0-7879-78973

Library of Congress Cataloging-in-Publication Data

Hale, Judith A.
  Outsourcing training and development : factors for success / Judith Hale.
    p. cm.
  Includes bibliographical references and index.
  ISBN 0-7879-7897-3 (alk. paper)
  1. Contracting out. 2. Employees—Training of. I. Title.
  HD2365.H35 2006
  658.3'124--dc22   05021189

Acquiring Editor: Matthew Davis   Editor: Rebecca Taff
Director of Development: Kathleen Dolan Davies   Manufacturing Supervisor: Becky Carreño
Production Editor: Dawn Kilgore   Editorial Assistant: Leota Higgins

Printed in the United States of America
Printing   10   9   8   7   6   5   4   3   2   1

Contents

List of Figures

CD-ROM Contents

Preface

This book is in response to the increasing interest in outsourcing training. The term "outsourcing" can evoke strong emotions, as it is associated with the relocation or elimination of jobs. Ironically, training departments have contracted with vendors for services for years, but did not call it outsourcing. The term outsourcing was originally used to describe organizations that chose to contract with other firms to provide necessary transactional services, such as payroll. Today, firms are outsourcing both staff and non-staff functions, including legal services, product distribution, customer support, telemarketing, and the like. This book, however, is just about outsourcing training, whether it be the whole function, key training processes, or major projects.

I was asked to write this book because of my experience helping organizations qualify suppliers and after market partners, such as distributors and product support. I also bring more than twenty-five years of experience as someone to whom organizations contracted for services, such as the design and development of technical training curriculum and certification. In writing this book, I have drawn on the experience of buyers and sellers of training services. This book is meant to help managers be better consumers of outsourcing services as they relate to training, and I hope it will help consulting firms become better providers of training products and services. The ideas in the book will be helpful to organizations that are contemplating outsourcing training or are currently in a relationship with a service provider and want guidance on how to improve that relationship.

AUDIENCE FOR THE BOOK

The primary audiences for this book are experienced HRD and training managers who are responsible for:

- Staffing
- Identifying and delivering training services
- Deciding what services to outsource
- Working with procurement to specify sourcing requirements
- Identifying and selecting external resources
- Managing contracts with external resources

The secondary audiences are (1) procurement and purchasing professionals who prepare requests for qualification (RFQs) and requests for proposals (RFPs) and specify contract terms and (2) contract managers who monitor contract deliverables and compliance.

ACKNOWLEDGMENTS

Some very special people played a major role in helping make this book possible. They painstakingly read the first draft of every chapter and added insights, examples, and guidance. They directed me to numerous articles in newspapers and on websites. They took the time to tell me about their experience as a buyer or seller of training services. They include:

Chellie Cameron, CPA, Manager of Airport Administration, Washington Dulles International Airport

Roger Chevelier, Director of Certification, ISPI

Tony DeSalvo, Independent Sales Trainer

Pierce Frels, Service Training, Certification Consultant, Product Support Division, Caterpillar Inc.

Linda Golhke, Esq., International Transactional Lawyer

Doug Harward, CEO and Managing Partner, The Exceleration Group and Co-Founder of TrainingOutsourcing.com

Dave Haskett, Project Manager, Camber Corporation, a provider of management and decision support, technical services, and products to government agencies

Sam Herrin, Executive Vice President of Research and Consulting, Intrepid Learning Solutions

William Horton, President, and Katherine Horton, Vice President, William Horton Consulting, Inc.

Anne Marie Laures, Manager of Learning Services, Walgreens

Daniel Messick, Strategic Planning Manager, Sales Training Division, Imaging Systems Group, Canon U.S.A. Inc.

Jim Momsen, Product Instructor, Catalyst International, Inc.

Leah Nelson, VNU Learning, Inc.

Craig Polak, Performance Consultant, Information Technology Training, Allstate Insurance Company

Mike Pusateri, CPA, CFO, Steller Recognitions Division of Dynamic Design

Ingo Schaefer, MBA, President of S&B, Inc.

Ken Silber, Professor, Northern Illinois University

Janice Simons, Director, Global Learning and Development, Johnson Controls, Controls Division

Harvey Singh, CEO of Instancy, Inc., and co-founder of www.TrainingOutsourcing.com

Jason Sprunk, Manager, Learning Solutions, Learning & Development, Tellabs Operations, Inc.

Marilyn Steffel, Corporate Manager, L&D, Molex Corporation

Brenda Sugrue, Senior V.P., Research, ASTD

Colleen Van Hoene, Manager, Terminal Concessions and Services, Metropolitan Washington Airports Authority

Charline Wells, Program Manager, Corporate Education, Training and Development, Sandia National Laboratories

Fred Wells, Vice President of Marketing, Mountain Bell; retired

I was fortunate to have the continued confidence of Kathleen Dolan Davies and Matt Davis of Pfeiffer, whose support made this book possible.

Special thanks go to Karen Kroczek and Grace Spitz for their help with the research, and Bonnie Grabenhofer and Gay Bruhn of Partners in Learning, for their help with editing and graphics.

Introduction

*T*his book has stories, examples, and guidelines to help managers, whether they be from training, HRD, procurement, finance, or the line organization, more fully understand the variables that lead to successful and unsuccessful relationships with external resources. The book, however, does not present cookie-cutter formulas for how to outsource. Instead, the ideas and guidelines are meant to serve as guides, not prescribe what to do, as the decision to outsource is too complex. It is a decision that should be made with input from many different vested parties, including training professionals, procurement, and line management. The stories of what organizations have done (or not done), guidelines, and checklists are meant to help readers:

- Determine if and how outsourcing would be of benefit
- Clarify what type of external resources they require
- Determine what they expect of external resources
- Specify what they require in terms of program deliverables, reports, quality assurance, risk management, and reporting relationships
- Determine their level of readiness to outsource, ranging from managing the T&D function as a whole to coordinating specific process elements
- Consider contractual elements that best protect their interests
- Collaborate effectively with all of the functions involved in outsourcing decisions

TERMS AND DEFINITIONS

Throughout this book terms are used, such as business model, contracting, outsourcing, partnering, sourcing, and vendors. Each of these terms is briefly defined here. Terms that are unique to a chapter will be defined in the chapter.

Business model[1] is the method by which organizations plan on increasing profits, improving market share, or fulfilling their social mandate. It includes the manner in which the organization will develop and provide products and services. Outsourcing is an example of a business model for increasing profits by improving the management of costs, reducing headcount, and avoiding investing in the capability or capacity of the training function. It is also a method for developing and providing products and services to internal clients and external customers.

Contracting is the process of formalizing a relationship with an external resource.

Outsourcing is entering into a long-term relationship with an external resource so as to leverage the capabilities and capacity of that resource. Outsourcing is done to better respond to demands for learning solutions that are technology based, manage training's costs, decrease cycle time, accelerate development and delivery, and avoid investment in developing the training function. Outsourcing may result in the elimination, relocation, or creation of jobs. At a minimum it forces the organization to assume new roles for the relationship to be successful.

Local or near sourcing is the use of external resources located close to the organization's headquarters. The use of nearby training resources is usually done to contribute to local economic development or assure better oversight and coordination. Organizations that have made public commitments to the economic development of the local community outsource to local training firms. Local sourcing may also allow people who have lost their jobs to find employment with the firm to whom their training function was outsourced.

Off shoring is sometimes used as a synonym for outsourcing; however, it refers to where the external resources are located in comparison to the organization's headquarters and the training function specifically. Off shoring is entering into a relationship with an external resource that is located in a country other than that of the address of the organization's headquarters. Offshore vendors are often selected on the basis of technological capability and lower costs.

Partnering is a term used to describe a relationship with an external training resource that is based on sharing accountabilities, responsibilities, and risks. An outsourcing relationship should be one of a partnership.

Sourcing is the process of identifying and selecting external resources that can fulfill one's requirements.

Vendors (external resources) are training firms that provide personnel, services, and product. Vendors are classified as:

- *Exclusive vendors*—external resources that are sole sources. They do not have to compete with other vendors for the right to provide specific services or products. Their relationship with the organization may or may not be considered one of outsourcing.
- *Preferred vendors*—external resources that have been pre-qualified as suppliers of specific services or products. Their relationship with the organization may or may not be considered one of outsourcing.
- *Tier-one vendors*—the primary vendors through which all other external training resources subcontract. Tier-one vendors can operate as general contractors, management agents, brokers, full-service providers, or program managers. Organizations outsource to tier-one vendors.
- *Tier-two vendors*—subcontractors to tier-one vendors and may provide general or specialized services.
- *Tier-three vendors*—subcontractors to tier-two vendors. They usually provide very specialized or discrete services or products.

HOW THE BOOK IS ORGANIZED

The book has eight chapters. Each chapter contains examples, guidelines, tools, tips, common missteps, and suggestions on where to learn more. There is a CD-ROM disk containing all of the job aids and templates.

Chapter 1. Outsourcing: A Business and Economic Model

This chapter is about the market forces that are pressuring organizations to consider outsourcing all or some of their training. The premise behind this chapter is that the reader should have some basic understanding of how economic drivers can influence the decisions of executive management. It lays out the argument for and against outsourcing the whole training and development function, compared to limited roles such as development and delivery.

Chapter 2. Identifying the Need

This chapter describes the overall process of deciding to outsource from the buyer's perspective. The premise is that effective outsourcing is based on a well-form process of being clear on the need, selecting an appropriate partner, and managing the relationship. It explains the different needs organizations have that they hope to address through outsourcing.

Chapter 3. Assessing Capacity and Capability

This chapter is about evaluating the training function's current capability and capacity to meet the organization's need for products and services. The premise is that the decision to outsource can be based on augmenting, supplementing, or replacing the current training function's capabilities.

Chapter 4. Selecting the Outsourcing Firm

The focus of this chapter is on selecting an outsourcing firm. The premise is that the training function should follow a selection process, decide what services it wants to buy, identify the criteria it will use to select an outsourcing firm, and determine what information it wants to solicit from potential firms. The chapter describes the benefits of issuing a request for qualification before the request for a proposal.

Chapter 5. Contracting

The focus of this chapter is on the phase when the training function works with its legal, procurement, and finance departments and the outsourcing firm to develop the contract and any required addenda. The premise is that the process of developing the agreement requires the expertise of the legal department working in collaboration with the training function to assure the language of the contract supports the intent of the organization and allows for changes to meet unanticipated needs.

Chapter 6. Starting Up

The focus of this chapter is on the phase during which the training function and outsourcing firm put plans and protocols in place for working together. This premise is that the foundation for an effective partnership requires the two groups to decide in advance how they will interface, communicate, and resolve disputes.

Chapter 7. Managing the Relationship

The focus of this chapter is on the ongoing management of the relationship. This is the phase during which the organization's representative oversees the relationship and implements the management plan. It is also during this phase that both parties celebrate success, address changes, work through issues, and solve problems.

Chapter 8. Closing Out

This chapter is about how to end an agreement. The premise is that all relationships come to an end, even if they are to be reconstituted in a new agreement. This chapter addresses the transfer of intellectual and real property.

NOTE

1. To learn more about business models, check out Wikipedia, the free online encyclopedia, for an interesting description about the evolution of business models. It can be found online at http://en.wikipedia.org. Also check out www.askjeeves.com or www.google.com for the latest articles on the subject of business models, outsourcing in general, and outsourcing training in particular.

Chapter 1

Outsourcing

A Business and Economic Model

*T*his chapter is about what is driving the increased interest in outsourcing training. There are three major drivers—economic, technology, and training's past performance. The economic drivers are the number of potential buyers and providers of training goods and services, the number of dollars spent on training, and the amount of venture capital available to new consulting firms. According to the Bureau of Labor Statistics (BLS), there are more than 200,000 people employed in training and development and there are approximately 3,800 independent training consultants.[1] According to the U.S. Census Bureau, there are almost eighteen million sole proprietors and approximately two million partnerships and five million corporations in the United States.[2] Of those enterprises, more than a million have five hundred or more employees, and almost 600,000 have more than 10,000.

It is difficult to accurately establish the amount of money organizations spend on training, as the number differs depending on the source. What is known is that larger organizations spend more money on employee training and they develop and market training to their customers. According to *Business Week,* industry is spending approximately $63 billion annually on training[3] and an increasing proportion is being outsourced. According to the Exceleration Group, expenditures or the market size for training and development services in North America will exceed $120 billion in 2004. This includes an estimated $53 billion targeted for employee training expenditures (*Training,* October 2003) and approximately $65B for customer training.[4] This investment in training in turn is attracting private investors who are underwriting both new and established training firms.

The increased use of the intranet and the emergence of technology-based training is another factor driving outsourcing of training. Technology and web-based training have created a need for instructional designers and training managers who understand both technology and learning, a combination not traditionally found in the training function. Today, the team involved in the creation, delivery, and maintenance of training consists of highly skilled programmers, graphic artists, and instructional designers experienced with multimedia suite development tools and web-based technologies. Outsourcing firms are able to hire or subcontract with the full array of specialists required to produce technical training programs capable of being deployed by way of an intranet to workers dispersed all over the world.

Another driver is the failure of training departments to demonstrate value. Training functions struggle with knowing how to show that their programs contribute to their organization's goals, and the fact that they are considered fixed costs makes them vulnerable to cost-cutting measures. Some drivers are shown in Figure 1.1.

Figure 1.1. Economic and Marketplace Drivers

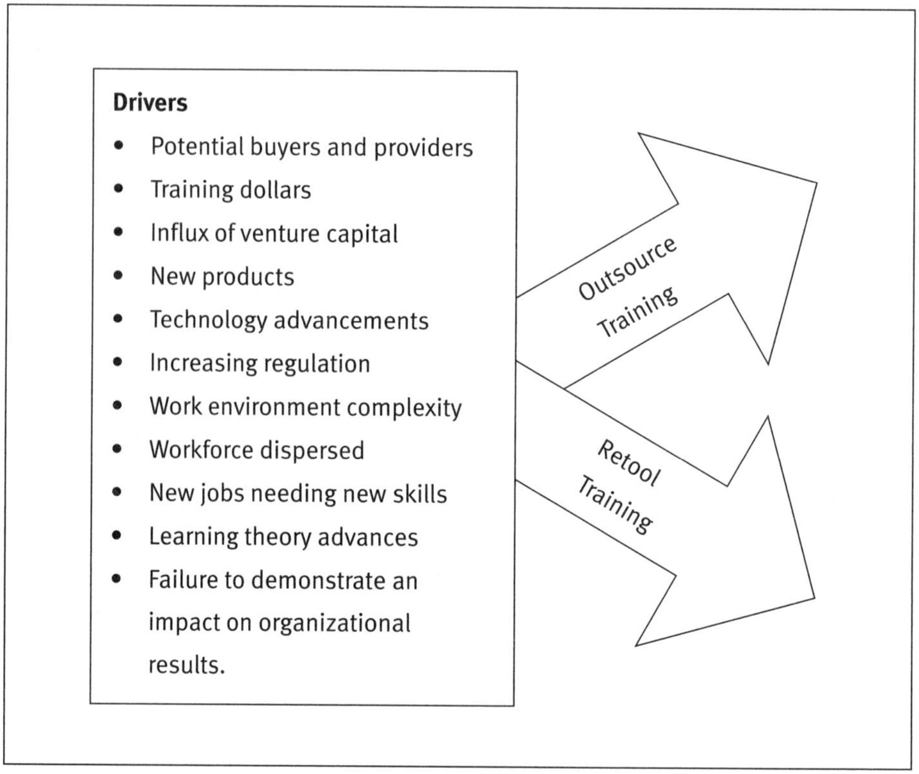

Drivers

- Potential buyers and providers
- Training dollars
- Influx of venture capital
- New products
- Technology advancements
- Increasing regulation
- Work environment complexity
- Workforce dispersed
- New jobs needing new skills
- Learning theory advances
- Failure to demonstrate an impact on organizational results.

Outsource Training

Retool Training

The investment in training is expected to increase because, according to the Bureau of Labor Statistics, organizations believe training develops skills, enhances productivity and quality of work, improves morale, and builds worker loyalty. According to the ASTD *2004 State of the Industry Report*, only 8 percent of their 213 benchmarked organizations do Level 4 evaluation (demonstrate the value gained from the investment in training); therefore, very few training departments can demonstrate that they add value to the organization.[5] Yet, businesses believe there is a direct correlation between the levels of investment in training and a firm's performance in the marketplace. Other factors that are driving the need for training are new products, technology advancements, and increasing regulation. The work environment is more complex, the workforce more dispersed, and there is a growing number of jobs in fields that are generating new knowledge.

At the same time the investment in training is growing, business and industry are being pressured to cut costs, reduce headcount, and avoid long-term liabilities like pension plans. As a result, organizations are looking for ways to meet the demand for training without hiring training specialists or investing in the development of their training function. A solution is to outsource.

A LITTLE HISTORY

Given that outsourcing is leveraging the capability and capacity of external resources long term, outsourcing today does not differ significantly from the large training contracts of the past. Major industries, particularly telecommunications, computing, automotive, and the military, have outsourced training services for years. The contracts were for millions of dollars and ran for a number of years, and contracting helped the organizations avoid hiring additional personnel. Similarly, sole proprietors and small and medium-size businesses have always outsourced their formal training and still do. Small and medium-size firms outsource through the local Better Business Bureaus, professional and trade associations, and community colleges. Large firms hire the expertise of consultants and training firms. Smaller firms tend to do basic skills training, and larger firms tend to do job skill training. So the attributes of leveraging external resources long term is not new.

Outsourcing Versus Contracting

The question becomes one of when is a relationship one of contracting versus outsourcing. Contracting, as a business model, is to use vendors to do special projects that are one-time events or supplement internal staff on specific assignments. Contractors are hired to augment training staff. Outsourcing, as a business model, is to substitute external resources for current employees. The goal is to either reduce the number of full-time employees (FTEs), avoid hiring more people, or replace current staff with outsourced personnel so they can be redeployed to other needed tasks that are perhaps less easily outsourced. The result is that the organization can either reduce or avoid increasing fixed costs. Here are some examples.

Outsourcing is the acquisition of external resources to perform current tasks or new ones so as to:

- Reduce headcount;
- Avoid the need to increase headcount; or
- Keep headcount the same but reassign them to tasks less easily outsourced.

Contracting is the acquisition of external resources to:

- Increase capability short-term or
- Augment staff's capability short term.

RESEARCH FIRM

Background: The firm has 8,000 employees and 2,000 contractors on site. The Training Department has thirty full-time employees. Last year the department delivered 116,00 training hours.

Contracting: If there were a project requiring someone with skills in developing a website or creating animated graphics for one or two programs, the department might contract with an individual or firm to do the work.

Outsourcing: If, however, the department wanted to deliver more training by way of websites or wanted the ability of add animated graphics to all future programs, it could either hire another employee (add an FTE), train one of its thirty trainers (redeploy the FTE), or outsource (not affect the FTE, yet expand capability).

THE SAME RESEARCH FIRM

Background: The firm spends about $1.5 million a year on tuition reimbursement. Currently one of the Training Department's thirty employees is assigned full-time to manage the tuition reimbursement program.

Outsource: The training manager wants to outsource tuition reimbursement because this would allow her to:

- Replace the person responsible for tuition reimbursement with someone with the skills that would be of greater value or
- Reassign the person responsible for tuition reimbursement to tasks he or she is already capable of doing but does not have the time to do.

Outsourcing lets the training manager still provide a service clients value, yet expand her department's capability by reassigning a resource to tasks of greater need.

Contracting: If the training manager only wanted to redeploy the person in charge of tuition reimbursement for a short time, perhaps six to nine months, at the end of which time the person would return to the old assignment, the training manager could just contract with someone.

POLE CLIMBING

Background: In the early 1980s the telephone and electric companies had a need to better train people to climb utility poles. All of the phone companies and utility companies got together and adopted a common set of standards for pole climbing.

　　Contract: The companies contracted with Southern Bell to develop a pole-climbing course they would all agree to use.

　　Outsource: The group then outsourced the delivery of the pole-climbing course to community colleges, allowing the companies to train about 75,000 people the first year.

　　Developing the course was a contract because it was a one-time event. All of the companies had the internal capability of developing the course, but wanted to avoid the cost of everyone doing their own program.

　　Delivery was an example of outsourcing, as the program would be needed annually, and if every company delivered the course they would have to either hire trainers or redeploy their current trainers. Delivery would affect FTEs.

CAR DEALERSHIPS

Background: There are approximately 21,000 independent car dealers and 55,000 independent used car dealers in the United States. A dealership might have a manager, assistant manager, sales manager, service manager, sales personnel, and service technicians. The number of sales personnel is based on the number of new cars delivered monthly. The industry standard is one sales person for every one hundred new cars delivered.

　　Outsourcing: Owners contract with independent consultants, such as Tony DeSalvo, to train their managers, sales managers, sales force, and service advisors. Tony has had a regular clientele since 1995. His programs include all aspects of the sales and sales management process, including negotiations, presentation, and recommending the right vehicle for the buyer. He also has a program for handling Internet sales. Outsourcing their training allows the dealerships to avoid hiring trainers.

　　Therefore, a relationship is one of a *contract* if it is

- For a single purpose or for a one-time project
- Has no impact on FTEs
- To acquire needed talent to bridge a specific gap

　　It is *outsourcing* if it affects FTEs and fixed costs by enabling the training function to:

- Reduce headcount and the related overhead
- Avoid increasing headcount

• Redeploy current headcount

Is a long-term solution for increasing the training function's capability and capacity

WHY OUTSOURCE

Organizations choose to outsource their training in deference to building internal capability and capacity based on a combination of business and training reasons, such as:

• Focus on core competencies
• Gain scalability of the workforce to avoid the need to lay people off
• Avoid long-term liability associated pensions and profit sharing
• Avoid the cost of building internal competence, especially within the training function
• Manage training costs
• Improve the revenue-per-employee ratio
• Acquire specific talent to support a new strategy or project

Focus on Core Competencies

The focus on core competencies is a newer business model in and of itself. Organizations are encouraged to ask: "What business are we in? What must we do and be better at to stay competitive in the marketplace? What functions are best done by other organizations that have that function as a core competency?" A result of focusing on core competencies is the elimination of those functions not seen as core to the business, including support or staff functions, also known as general and administrative or G&A. Support and staff functions are necessary for running the organization's infrastructure, but of little interest to customers unless they are inefficient and interfere with service delivery. The more common G&A functions being outsourced include:

• Accounts payable and receivable
• Payroll
• Compensation and benefits
• Information technology, especially the Human Resource Information Systems (HRIS)
• Legal services
• Public relations and communications

Depending on an organization's view of its core competencies, it may outsource its marketing, manufacturing, distribution, customer support, and product installation and repair.

Training is by definition a support function—particularly if it is viewed as a cost center that does not have a recognized value to the organization—and therefore susceptible to being outsourced. Just because training is not perceived as a core competency does not make it unimportant. It means the organization chooses to turn the responsibility over to an external firm that has training as its core competency. It wants a firm whose personnel are fluent in all aspects of training's processes, including design, development, delivery, and administration. The organization also wants an external resource with the latest technology and systems required to efficiently develop and deploy programs to employees wherever they are located.

Gain Scalability

Scalability is the ability to quickly downsize or grow in response to market demands. The telecom and high-technology industries experienced a significant economic downturn between 1999 and 2003. The automotive industry is cyclical. It goes through good times and bad times. Training departments are especially affected during bad times when organizations downsize. Training functions may lose the majority of their personnel, and even whole departments can be eliminated. Organizations are looking for ways to avoid the need to lay off people in the future. One response is the ongoing search of the right size. Another response is converting functions that are fixed costs or G&A to variable costs by contracting and outsourcing services. When a company decides to outsource all or part of a function, it can construct an agreement that can be adjusted annually, even quarterly, based on need. It becomes the outsourcing firm's dilemma as to how to retain and keep qualified personnel billable. The assumption is that outsourcing firms are better able to respond to changing marketplace demands because they have more than one customer and, therefore, have the ability to shift personnel to different customers' projects.

Avoid Long-Term Liability

The financial scandals experienced over the last few years resulted in the accounting profession revising its accounting standards. The new standards require firms to be more conservative in their projections as to what their long-term liabilities are related to employees' pension plans. They must more accurately account for costs that are considered overhead or fixed. The organizations must significantly increase their contributions to their retirement plans and must more carefully estimate how many employees will stay until retirement. Outsourcing is a way to avoid this liability.

Avoid Cost of Building Internal Competence

To meet the need for training requires organizations to invest in the training function's skills and technology. Training professionals must be proficient in instructional design, adult learning theory, the use of electronic authoring and delivery systems, and learning management systems (LMS). Organizations may be willing to invest in keeping their line workers current, but not staff. The debate becomes one of if and when to hire, what skill sets to hire, and what to outsource.

The federal government and the military in particular are mandated to use commercial services, instead of hiring personnel. They have developed a set of guidelines to help them weigh the economic and non-economic factors of hiring compared to outsourcing. The argument for hiring requires looking at the job, the expertise required to perform the job, the availability and market value of that expertise, and for how long the expertise will be required.[6] The guidelines suggest weighting the following:

- Costs
    - *Employment costs*—salaries and benefits. This cost can be significant once training professionals become vested in the organization's pension plan.
    - *Currency costs*—the cost to keep training professionals current in the subject and the technology. The knowledge base for some jobs is static; but it is ever-changing for training. The cost of staying current can be significant, and this cost exists for vendors as well.
    - *Learning curve*—the cost to bring a person up-to-speed should there be turnover. This includes knowledge of the organization (its people, products, and processes), content (learning objectives, concepts and rules, and examples), learning strategy (self-study, classroom, practice, simulations, and on-the-job training), projects (status, roles, schedules, and deliverables), learning technologies (LMS, authoring systems, testing software, and hosting capabilities and requirements), and administration (reporting requirements). This cost applies to training professionals and vendors.
- Job complexity
    - *Amount and variety of product or organizational knowledge required of the job*—the jobs performed by training professionals are becoming increasingly complex. One factor is the increasing reliance on technology to develop and deploy programs. The need to constantly develop new content also adds complexity.
- Marketplace
    - *Availability*—the number of people in the marketplace with the desired combination of knowledge and skills. Depending on the skills sought, they might be abundant and readily available, or they might be difficult to obtain. If the demand for a set of skills is short term, contracting may be the only option.

- *Competition*—the number of employment opportunities for training specialists and generalists. As more and more organizations move to e-learning and distance learning, the competition increases for certain skill sets and the cost for acquiring them increases.

- Risk management
  - *Safety*—the exposure to unsafe working conditions and the degree to which hiring or outsourcing will reduce, increase, or allow for better control over that exposure. Some work environments such as manufacturing and laboratories present workplace hazards. When contractors are on the premises, they must be trained in how to behave in those environments. The cost for training applies to both employees and contractors. When training is outsourced, training and liability costs are assumed by the vendor.

  - *Asset protection*—the access to privileged information or economic assets and the degree to which the relationship can be designed to reduce that access or mitigate loss. Training has access to the organization's plans, processes, and desires. Protecting that information can be considered very important. Whether the risk is higher when you outsource or retain the work internally is questionable.

  - *Confidentiality*—how it will be preserved should there be turnover. Signing confidentiality agreements applies to both employees and the outsource firm.

- Loyalty
  - Pertains to the risk of losing the intelligence or expertise should the person leave the organization or the vendor's employment. This is similar to the issues under the learning curve. People build relationships and gain institutional knowledge that can be abused or misapplied when employees and contractors become disgruntled.

Manage Training Costs and Improve Revenue Per Employee Ratio

One of the main arguments for outsourcing training is cost control. Organizations have a difficult time determining just what their training costs are. ASTD, the largest professional association representing the training industry, struggles with collecting valid metrics of what companies spend on training. A number of factors contribute to the confusion and lack of clarity; however, the main reason is the lack of agreement on what costs to include and how those costs are calculated. For example:

- Training is rarely centralized and not under a single budget, making it difficult to control costs. Most large organizations, even if their training function is centralized, have renegade trainers whose costs are rarely captured, much less managed.

- Training costs are classified under different headings in the budget.

- Managers hide training costs.

- Trainers have numerous titles, and their salaries may not be part of the training budget.

- There is no agreement on what costs to include, such as learners' time, facilities, travel, trainers' time, materials, tuition reimbursement, conference fees, professional continuing education, and so forth.

- There is no agreement on how to spread or allocate the cost of design and development across offerings.

- There are no agreed-on protocols for classifying and tracking training's indirect costs, such as for registration, record-keeping, material warehousing, and production.

When organizations outsource training, they are forced to place a value on it and manage it. They have to decide on deliverables, service levels, and a budget. The organization is then in a better position to monitor expenses.

The flip side of the cost coin is the inability of most training departments to demonstrate that they actually add value through measurable results that impact the bottom line. If value cannot be measured, the basic question that remains is whether it is cheaper to keep the training function in-house or outsource it.

Gain Access to Learning Technologies

The organization may expect to benefit in other ways as well by outsourcing training, such as:

- It may gain access to the latest technology and highly skilled specialists.

- It will avoid the need to invest in (1) the latest training software and hardware required to support the development and delivery training and (2) the ongoing development of its training personnel.

Other Benefits

Organizations may reap other benefits as a result of outsourcing. For example, investors monitor a company's revenue-per-employee ratio. This ratio is improved when the number of full-time employees (FTEs) goes down. Eliminating support functions collectively can reduce headcount sufficiently to make the ratio more attractive to investors. However, eliminating the training function alone will probably not affect the ratio significantly, as training's percentage of the overall G&A costs may be small compared to the overall number of employees.

Outsourcing may result in the organization engaging the services of fewer external resources by contracting with an exclusive vendor or a tier-one vendor. This strengthens the organization's ability to negotiate lower costs and makes management of the external resource easier. A side benefit is a reduction on accounts payable transactions.

TOOL 1.1: GUIDELINES FOR CLARIFYING WHY TO OUTSOURCE

These guidelines are intended to help you to think about why you might want to or are already outsourcing some or parts of the training function. If you are considering outsourcing all or just specific responsibilities of the training function, meet with your key stakeholders and answer the following questions. The collective answers are intended to help you begin the process of weighing all of the variables. The subsequent chapters will add other points for consideration.

1. What is your organization's business model? What is its approach to delivering goods and services to the marketplace? Does outsourcing play a role?

2. What is your organization's position on G&A or fixed costs? Does it have a plan for reducing G&A costs or converting fixed costs to variable costs? What proportion of these costs is attributable to training?

3. What problem do you think outsourcing will solve? Is it:

   a. The desire to direct more attention to the core business?

   b. The desire to be able to downsize or grow quickly?

   c. The need to better identify the true cost of training and manage it appropriately?

   d. The need to expand the function's ability to leverage technology?

4. What is your current situation?

   a. How many people make up the training function?

   b. What is your average annual training budget?

   c. Do you expect the demand for training to grow?

   d. Is there an expectation that training should do more, offer different services, or do work differently? If so, in what way?

   e. How do you measure training results? Is it just an activity, or can you show that it improves individual and organizational performance?

This information will help you build a baseline against which you can better evaluate the potential benefits of outsourcing, potential external resources, and the effectiveness of the relationship once you should decide to outsource.

WHAT IS OUTSOURCED

As a business model, outsourcing can be applied to the training function as a whole, key processes, or major programs. At whatever level it is applied, it is a purposeful decision to not hire or further invest in the training function's capability and capacity. It is a decision about how to best use internal resources. What is outsourced may include:

- Operating the whole function
- Developing and managing training's administrative activities
- Designing and developing courses and courseware
- Designing and developing e-learning courseware
- Maintaining servers and hosting e-learning courseware
- Managing and providing course facilitation

One of the better-documented examples of outsourcing the whole training function is Nortel, the Canadian Company.[7] Nortel's reasons for outsourcing its training function were to:

- Focus on its core competencies
- Gain scalability
- Better manage training costs

These are the same arguments used by other organizations choosing to outsource the function. Nortel's annual training budget was approximately $178 million. By outsourcing, Nortel established a training budget based on specified deliverables. It essentially eliminated the training function. What remained were executive leadership and administrative staff. It gained the ability to better manage its training costs and determine whether the expenditure positively affected the company's performance.

Outsourcing Parts of the Function

Another approach is to outsource selected areas or disciplines and to keep those areas that the function excels in. Training departments, just like whole companies, have strengths and weaknesses. Older, more established departments may have started out developing and delivering classroom training. Another training function may have started with the information technology (IT) department. Another may have only arranged to lease off-the-shelf programs. Today, these departments may be expected to provide consultation on performance issues, recommend the best combination of electronic delivery systems, manage learning management systems (LMS), modularize training content so it can be stored and accessed through a learning content management system (LCMS), track continuing education units so employees can retain their certifications, maintain a server or an intranet to host online learning programs, and more. The expectations of the function exceed either its capability or capacity to respond with current staff. In this situation, outsourcing may be a responsible solution.

What Cannot Be Outsourced

The one responsibility that cannot nor should it be outsourced is leadership of the function. The organization still has to retain responsibility and accountability for identifying developmental needs, deciding what skills to develop versus hire, and allocating funds for development. Senior management is responsible for talent development, management, and retention, as well as for ensuring that the training has the desired result.

Figure 1.2 shows what is outsourced and what is not.

Figure 1.2. What Is and Is Not Outsourced

Not Outsourced	Outsourced
• Leadership of training function	• Operating the whole function
• Processes that are training department strengths	• Administration
	• Course development
	• E-learning course development
	• E-learning hosting
	• Facilitation/delivery

TOOL 1.2: GUIDELINES FOR DECIDING WHAT TO OUTSOURCE

One of the harder decisions is about what or how much to outsource, as the implications can be significant. The following questions are intended to start you in the process of identifying what your training function currently does or does not do and what you might want to outsource to expand the function's capability or capacity. Subsequent chapters deal with the question of what to outsource in greater detail. Meet with your key stakeholders and begin to discuss the following topics:

1. What are you thinking about outsourcing?

   a. The whole function?

   b. Administrative activities?

   c. Course development in general?

   d. E-learning course development?

   e. Facilitation and delivery?

2. As you go over the list above, what specifically did you have in mind for items b through e?

3. How do you think the organization will benefit if you outsource?

4. What do you see as being different as a result of outsourcing?

5. If you were to outsource all or some of the training function, how would the results be different from what the organization is experiencing now?

This information will help you be clear in your expectations and what exactly you want from an outsourcing relationship.

WHAT THE RELATIONSHIP LOOKS LIKE

The format of a relationship between a buyer and an outsourcing firm depends on the models used by purchasing, procurement, or the contacting department. Some purchasing departments like preferred vendors; others like the tiered vendor model. Most want to reduce the number of vendors the organization has. Their reasons include reducing the number of transactions handled by accounts payable, the number of security clearances that have to be done, and the number of badges that have to be prepared to allow outsiders access to the property. Having more vendors makes for more administrative work.

The outsourcing firm can take on more roles than that of a training resource. Depending on the relationship, it may function as:

- A sourcing agent that identifies and contracts with independent consultants and firms to provide services. As a sourcing agent it may charge a finder's fee or an administrative fee. Sourcing agents usually provide no oversight of the work being done. However, they can shield the organization from employment taxes and benefit costs because they can hire the independent contractors as employees.

- A general contractor that coordinates the work of subcontractors. In this model the outsourcing firm provides oversight and direction. The subcontractors do not become employees of the general contractor.

- A tier-one contractor through which all other contractors bill their services. Tier-one contractors may or may not provide oversight, and the tier-two and -three vendors do not become employees of the tier-one contractor.

The differences between these relationships are subtle but important, as they are about where responsibility rests, who provides oversight, what the employment status is of vendors, and how billing is handled. Large consulting firms, such as Accenture, Exceleration Group, Intrepid, Productivity Point, Raytheon, RWD, and others, may operate as full-service providers or as general contractors. They provide qualified personnel and oversight and may be responsible for any employment taxes and benefits. When they are full-service providers, the personnel assigned to the contract are employees of the outsourcing firm.

Other outsourcing firms operate as sourcing agents. Manpower, for example, is a sourcing agent that hires independent consultants based on the requirements of the contract. The consultants become employees of Manpower, are eligible for health benefits, and can earn paid vacation time. The buyer is responsible for oversight and supervision. Source One is also a sourcing agent; however, the personnel it provides remain independent contractors. Source One provides some oversight, but its buyers are responsible for supervision. PriceWaterhouseCooper, the firm to which Nortel outsourced its whole training function, operated as a sourcing agent.

Other organizations prefer the tiered model to reduce administration costs. Large organizations may have as many as four thousand qualified vendors whose invoices they process monthly. The tiered model reduces this administrative burden and allows accounts payable to avoid adding FTEs. However, the organizations usually place requirements on who is eligible to be tier-one, -two, or -three vendors. For example, the Metropolitan Washington Airports Authority (Authority), the organization that owns and operates National and Dulles Airports, outsources its organization development (OD) and performance management services. The vendor operates both as a preferred contractor and a tier-one vendor. The Authority identified other firms that are eligible to operate as tier-two vendors to do training on subjects such as coaching and how to use proprietary software and consulting such as process reengineering and outplacement. The Authority has strict rules on who is eligible for the tier-two and tier-three contracts. Specifically, the Authority requires that 25 percent of the contract dollars go to local disadvantaged business enterprises, known as LDBEs. Local is defined as being located within one hundred miles of the airports. Disadvantaged are women and minority owned enterprises. The tier-one vendor in OD processes all of the invoices submitted by these tier-two vendors for their services.

TOOL 1.3: GUIDELINES FOR
SURFACING OUTSOURCING CONSIDERATIONS

The following questions are intended to surface the group's biases about the type of outsourcing firm it wants to consider. Meet with your stakeholders and discuss the following questions:

1. Does it matter where the outsourcing firm is located? If so, why?

2. Have we made any promises to employees, customers, investors, or the community that might affect the type of outsourcing firm we use? What are those promises?

3. How much control do we want to have over the work products and how they are produced? Why?

4. How would we rate our project management, instructional design skills, and learning technology capabilities? Would our strengths and weaknesses influence the type of outsourcing firm that is best for us? If so, how?

IMPLICATIONS

The press and media report regularly on outsourcing. *The Wall Street Journal,* for example, publishes a regular series on the topic. The position the press and media take is not always positive, and they often interchange the terms "outsourcing" and "off shoring." However, they raise issues about the long-term economic and social implications of outsourcing. Therefore, as you weigh the pros and cons of outsourcing training, you should be prepared to answer questions about loss of jobs, company intelligence, and loyalty. You may be asked questions about if and how the decision to outsource might affect the local, national, and global economy.

Some training functions that have seen much of their work outsourced believe that outsourcing is creative accounting at best or management's feeble attempt at dealing with an issue that they do not otherwise know how to handle, such as how to control the cost of developing their people. The line organization, in turn, may see outsourcing as a reasonable response to training's inability to manage its costs and prove the value of its services. Whatever position you take, outsourcing can transform the training function. It forces the organization to place a value on people development. It gives the organization access to highly skilled specialists and the latest web-based and technology-based delivery systems with minimal investment. It puts in place management and accounting systems that allow for better allocation and tracking of costs. It can bring discipline to a function that historically has avoided being accountable for the impact of its programs.

MISSTEPS AND OVERSIGHTS

It is important that when organizations and external resources begin the process of entering into a business relationship they base it on a solid foundation. Here are some of the oversights both sides make that can jeopardize the success of the relationship:

- They are unclear or have not fully examined the reasons for wanting a relationship.
- They fail to establish a baseline against which they can fairly evaluate the relationship.
- They lack a culture of a long-term relationship, and instead think applying a project-oriented model is all that is needed.
- They overlook the long-term economic implications of their decisions, whether on the organization, the outsourcing firm, or local businesses.
- They focus on the activity of training rather than the measurable results necessary to improve the bottom line.
- They fail to use legally binding contracts that adequately define and document work expectations and requirements.

This list will be continued in subsequent chapters.

SUMMARY

Outsourcing is the decision to leverage the capability and capacity of external resources long term so the organization can (1) focus its internal resources on those parts of the business most important to customers; (2) structure the training department for greater scalability; (3) control or reduce training costs, including employees' salaries and benefits; and (4) gain access to training technologies. The relationship can take different formats that address how oversight, employment costs, and billing are to be handled and who is responsible.

Figure 1.3, The Engagement Process, shows how the remainder of the book is organized. Each of the following chapters is dedicated to one of the phases in the engagement process.

WHERE TO LEARN MORE

Here are some resources to learn more about outsourcing training:

ASTD hosts a number of annual conferences. Both the winter ASTD TechKnowledge Conference and the annual ASTD International Conference and Expo have large expositions where vendors of training products and services display their abilities. ASTD now offers a conference just on the topic of outsourcing. All of the conferences offer educational sessions for training managers, training specialists, and instructional designers. Also check out ASTD's monthly journal, *T&D*, for relevant articles. ASTD's website is www.astd.org.

Phase 1: Identifying the Need	Phase 2: Assessing Capacity and Capability	Phase 3: Selecting the Outsourcing Firm	Phase 4: Contracting	Phase 5: Starting Up	Phase 6: Managing the Relationship	Phase 7: Closing Out

Determine client's needs
a. shorten cycle times
b. deliver more training
  • regulation
  • turnover
c. provide greater access to training
d. test learners' knowledge
e. report on workforce capability
f. expanding learning audience
g. honor past and future commitments
Determine criticality and priority
	Assess strengths
	a. credibility and trust
	b. capacity
	c. capability
	d. knowledge and skills
	e. resources
	f. work processes
	g. standards
	Assess weaknesses
	Conduct job task analysis
	a. by role
	b. by task and skill
		Set the baseline
		Define roles and responsibilities
		Define the requirements
		Define the selection criteria
		Recruit potential outsourcing firms
		Issue the RFQ
		Issue the RFP
		Convene the panel and decide
			Prepare the contract
			Draft master agreement
			Determine scope of work
			a. deliverables
			b. reporting requirements
			c. problem resolution
			d. quality and service level
			e. timeliness and termination
			Draft addenda
			Agree on terms and conditions
			a. Accountability
			b. Budget
			c. Fees
			d. Flexibility
			e. Quality statement
			f. Service level statement
				Build contract profile
				Set up governance process
				Develop management plan and schedule
				Create communication protocols
				Develop document standards and controls
				Agree on deliverable standards
				Identify intellectual property
				Create transition plan
				Create dispute resolution process
					Provide oversight
					Implement the plan and protocols
					Share expectations and agree on goals
					Communicate
					Stay current with needs
					Measure and report results
					Celebrate success
					Improve processes
						Notify about termination
						Transfer intellectual property
						Return physical property
						Reconcile financial obligations
						Terminate clearances, codes
						Execute final performance review
						Orient the training function

Figure 1.3. The Engagement Process

The International Society for Performance Improvement (ISPI) focuses on measuring results and improving performance. It has annual and fall conferences that work toward these ends. To learn more about measured results, go to www.ispi.org: Got results section.

The Outsourcing Training website at www.outsourcingtraining.com reports the latest outsourcing activities and facts and figures. This website is sponsored by the large consulting firms.

VNU Learning hosts two annual conferences, one in the winter and one in the fall. They are called "Training" followed by the year. Both conferences have large expositions where vendors of training products and services display their abilities. The conferences also offer educational sessions for training managers, training specialists, and instructional designers. VNU also hosts a summer Training Director's Forum, a smaller, more intimate conference for training managers. VNU publishes a monthly journal called *Training*. The website is www.vnulearning.com.

NOTES

1. The Bureau of Labor Statistics has a website with the latest employment figures. The information referenced in this book is based on BLS 04 on HR Employment at www.bls.gov/oco/ocos021.htm.

2. The last published U.S. Census was in 2001. To find more statistics about all industries in the United States, check the website www.census.gob/epcd/susb/2001/us/US. Bizstats is another website that has information about businesses in North America. It is located at www.bizstats.com/businesses.htm.

3. *Business Week*'s Online Magazine Dated January 10, 2000, states: "In 1999, the amount of private-venture capital pouring into education quadrupled, to $3.3 billion. . . And in 2000, it . . . will swell to at least $4 billion. . . . The $63-billion corporate-training market, for instance, has always been dominated by private firms. Most training is done in-house, but companies are increasingly outsourcing it . . . overall corporate training is growing 5 percent a year, the outsourcing piece is growing 10 percent to 12 percent a year. . . ." According to *Business Week*, the total education market in 2000 was $780 billion. This includes elementary and high schools, community colleges and trade schools, and higher education.

4. Outsourcing Training Facts and Figures. See www.trainingoutsourcing.com/exec_factsfigures.asp.

5. ASTD conducts benchmarking studies and publishes them in its annual industry report.

6. A-76 Guidelines. The basic argument to hire is based on what is referred to as the A-76 Guidelines. Even though these guidelines may not directly apply to profit and not-for-profit enterprises, they can help formulate the argument for and against outsourcing. Here is a website to learn more about these guidelines: www.whitehouse.gov/omb. Once at the home page, go to the section titled circulars.

7. To learn more about the Nortel experience, go to www.trainingoutsouring.com.

Phase 1: Identifying the Need	Phase 2: Assessing Capacity and Capability	Phase 3: Selecting the Outsourcing Firm	Phase 4: Contracting	Phase 5: Starting Up	Phase 6: Managing the Relationship	Phase 7: Closing Out
Determine client's needs	Assess strengths	Set the baseline	Prepare the contract	Build contract profile	Provide oversight	Notify about termination
a. shorten cycle times	a. credibility and trust	Define roles and responsibilities	Draft master agreement	Set up governance process	Implement the plan and protocols	Transfer intellectual property
b. deliver more training	b. capacity	Define the requirements	Determine scope of work	Develop management plan and schedule	Share expectations and agree on goals	Return physical property
• regulation	c. capability	Define the selection criteria	a. deliverables	Create communication protocols	Communicate	Reconcile financial obligations
• turnover	d. knowledge and skills	Recruit potential outsourcing firms	b. reporting requirements	Develop document standards and controls	Stay current with needs	Terminate clearances, codes
c. provide greater access to training	e. resources	Issue the RFQ	c. problem resolution	Agree on deliverable standards	Measure and report results	Execute final performance review
d. test learners' knowledge	f. work processes	Issue the RFP	d. quality and service level	Identify intellectual property	Celebrate success	Orient the training function
e. report on workforce capability	g. standards	Convene the panel and decide	e. timeliness and termination	Create transition plan	Improve processes	
f. expanding learning audience	Assess weaknesses		Draft addenda	Create dispute resolution process		
g. honor past and future commitments	Conduct job task analysis		Agree on terms and conditions			
Determine criticality and priority	a. by role		a. Accountability			
	b. by task and skill		b. Budget			
			c. Fees			
			d. Flexibility			
			e. Quality statement			
			f. Service level statement			

Figure 2.1. The Engagement Process, Phase 1: Identifying the Need

Chapter 2
Identifying the Need

*T*his chapter introduces the process of outsourcing from the buyer's perspective, but the focus is on determining what factors are driving the need for training or for the function to perform differently. The process begins with determining the business need and ends with the disengagement. It can be applied to outsourcing the training function as a whole, the design and development of instructor-led courseware and e-learning solutions, and the operation of training's infrastructure. At whatever level it is applied, the process is intended to facilitate purposeful decisions about whether or not to hire, whether and how to invest in the training function's capability and capacity, and how to best use internal and external resources (see Figure 2.1, The Engagement Process, on the facing page).

Unfortunately, outsourcing decisions are frequently driven by senior management's desire to cut costs or shift them from fixed to variable costs by lowering the internal headcount. In this situation, outsourcing decisions may have little to do with learning. Also, senior management are rarely the primary clients of the training function, which is why it is so important to involve them in the needs assessment process; otherwise training professionals and their main clients may never understand why the decision was made to outsource, such as in response to a merger, acquisition, or new market opportunity.

DETERMINE CLIENTS' NEEDS

The needs are the performance requirements of the training function, what it must do and deliver to satisfy the expectations of its internal clients and the organization as a whole. Training functions are expected to develop and deliver training, make it accessible to learners throughout the enterprise, assess people's learning, and maintain records about learners and their training history. Depending on how rapidly the client's needs are growing or changing, the question is "What else must the training function do or do differently to satisfy

27

the need?" The answers will help establish the framework for deciding what specifically to outsource. The needs training functions seek to address by building internal capability or leveraging the capabilities of others include:

- Shorten cycle times
- Deliver more training
- Provide greater access to training
- Test learners' knowledge
- Report on the workforce's capability, readiness, and regulatory compliance
- Service an expanding learning audience
- Honor past and future commitments

These needs compound on one another. They are not discrete. All of them require more sophisticated skills and access to the latest learning technology and tools.

Shorten Cycle Times

The question is whose cycle time is to be shortened. The answer is both the training function's time to create courseware and the learners' time to develop proficiency. Clients are demanding that training be available when they want it. This means that the training function has to produce it on time and just in time. There are a number of approaches to shortening development cycle times. One is to adopt a minimalist philosophy, whereby the training function only builds just enough and nothing more. This philosophy is based on giving people only what they need, or focusing on the critical 20 percent and putting the rest in a job aid. Some training groups use rapid prototyping and an increased reliance on performance support tools. Another approach is to reduce content to reusable learning objectives to gain the ability to rapidly build training by leveraging that which has already been created and focusing attention on what is new. Whatever approach is taken, it will require an investment in expertise and technology.

To shorten the time it takes learners to become proficient in a task requires the training to be relevant, of high fidelity, include opportunities to practice, and give people feedback. High fidelity means the training examples and demonstrations are as close to the task as possible. For example, learners may be required to do case studies, exercises, and role plays using information, equipment, and systems they would normally have access to on the job. Practice sessions would be interactive, with a way for the learner to receive feedback, and the course materials might incorporate video, audio, animation, and graphics. Relevant, high fidelity, effective training requires skill in conducting job task analyses and in converting that information into well-designed learning events.

e-Learning courses are frequently shorter than classroom courses covering similar content—another way to shorten learners' time. However, e-learning solutions require training professionals to have skills in building electronic performance support systems and a deep understanding of all of the components for web-based and computer-based training. e-Learning also requires skill in using authoring systems, computer generated graphics, and animation software—at a minimum. The question then becomes whether or not to buy these skills or build them internally.

LEVERAGE INDUSTRY TRAINING

The Need
The manufacturer is experiencing a shortage of qualified technicians due to retirements and international expansion. The company estimates it will need to train as many as 45,000 in the next three to five years. The training function conducted a job task analysis of the technician's job. It determined that technicians must know the core systems common across all equipment families, such as hydraulics and electronics, and the operations of specific pieces of equipment.

The Solution
A trade association had a complete curriculum on hydraulics, drive systems, electronics, and more. The manufacturer decided to leverage the association's curriculum so it could just focus on building training that was product specific.

Deliver More Training

Change Drives Training. Whenever organizations adopt new technology or upgrade their technology and improve their work processes, they put in motion the need to reorient and retool the workforce. The addition of new products and services or changes to existing ones also triggers the need to update employees, customers, and the sales, distribution, and support partners. The irony is that old systems, equipment, and products do not go away. Workers have to support the old and the new, and the training function is expected to help them do both. This in turn requires the training function to build, maintain, and support databases, catalogues, and dictionaries of learning content so it can be rapidly accessed and modified as needed. The result is an increasing demand for learning management (LMS) and learning content management systems (LCMS) to document, house, and make content accessible. These systems require trainers to acquire even more skills in the use of technology for them to be useful.

ELECTRONICS MANUFACTURER

Background

The company makes small electronic components for original equipment manufacturers. The company has facilities in the Americas, Europe, and the Far East. Worldwide it has 21,000 employees with twenty-two in the training department. The annual training budget runs between $8M to $10M. The breakout of the department's staff is

- Corporate Training and Development (1)
- Regional training managers (4)
- Assistant regional training manager in the Far East (1)
- Product trainers (3)
- Systems training manager (1)
- Systems regional trainers (4)
- System sales/statistics trainer (1)
- Inside sales corporate trainers/including other responsibilities (2)
- Plant trainers (official—no other duties) (2)
- Administrative support for training (3 full-time—1 in corporate, 1 in the Americas, 1 in the Far East)

The Situation

The company's products are used by many different industries, which requires the people in manufacturing, sales, and customer support to stay current. The company invested in an enterprise-wide database system to manage information needs about product development, sales, marketing, accounting, and human resources.

The Need

The training function found it had a need to accelerate the rate at which it could develop technical product training and training on how to use the new enterprise-wide system. It decided to outsource the development of its custom technical and industry training by utilizing internal product trainers and product managers as subject-matter experts. It outsourced the development to a firm that had a proven capability in creating web-based training on technical subjects requiring computer graphics and animation.

Regulation Drives Training and Documentation. Local, state, national, and professional groups impose standards and regulations on people engaged in the sale and delivery of specific goods and services. The regulating bodies are expecting employers and individual practitioners to document compliance with the regulations. The problem is compounded by the need to demonstrate that people are satisfying their continuing education and recertification requirements. Training and human resources (HR) are the groups most burdened with the demand to provide continuing education, testing, and then document compliance.

THE RESTAURANT CHAIN

Background

The chain had close to five hundred restaurants. Each one had a dining area, a sports bar, and a to-go window. Turnover of servers and bartenders ran from between 80 to 100 percent. The only formal training that the chain did was for restaurant managers and assistant managers. They in turn hired experienced chefs, waitresses, and bartenders. All other training was done on the job.

The Need

There was increasing number of lawsuits being reported in the restaurant industry as a whole about over-serving customers alcohol. The restaurant industry responded by advocating the certification of managers and bartenders. The insurance industry responded by reducing liability premiums for those restaurants that implemented a comprehensive responsible alcohol program. The chain decided to be proactive and push to get all bartenders and managers trained and certified in responsible alcohol service.

The Solution

Rather than hire trainers to deliver the program, the chain decided to outsource the training to the restaurant association, which, acting as a sourcing agent, provided qualified instructors to deliver the program and administer the certification exam.

The need for documentation spurred software companies to develop sophisticated learning management systems (LMS) and human resource information systems (HRIS). The acquisition of new sophisticated software systems in turn requires people to be trained in how to use and support them. The need to rapidly deliver training on changes and maintain accurate documentation about people's compliance with regulations forces the questions about how to do this cost-effectively. Training now has to be skilled in the use of LMS.

TRACKING CEUS

The Need

The firm had over 50,000 employees worldwide who were certified accountants. To retain their certifications they must earn a minimum number of continuing education units (CEUs) annually. If they fail to earn the minimum number of units, they are not allowed to do work under their own signature. Currently five full-time staff manage the record-keeping.

The Solution

The training function decided to locate a firm with the capability of tracking, documenting, and reporting compliance and non-compliance.

Turnover Drives Training. Some industries, such as hospitality, restaurants, and call centers, experience very high turnover. Turnover can even exceed 100 percent. Unfortunately, people cannot just step into today's jobs; they have to be trained on the company's processes, systems, products, and equipment. As a result, the cost of training new hires can be enormous, especially when it takes weeks to bring a person to a basic level of proficiency. Therefore, the training function has to be very efficient in how it prepares new hires for the job. The content has to be critical to the job and the practice has to be as similar to the job environment as possible. This ongoing need to bring people to proficiency quickly forces the training function to look for new ways to deliver courseware, ranging from self-study to instructor-led. The range of delivery options can incorporate web-based and computer-based training. Training functions should weigh the benefits of outsourcing delivery, including contracting with independent trainers to finding someone to host the training function's website.

Provide Greater Access to Training

Not only has the demand for training increased, but clients want to make it readily accessible. In the past, learners went to training. Today, training comes to learners at their place of work, at customers' locations, wherever products and equipment are being used, when traveling, and at home. Training functions have responded to the expectation that courses come to learners by making programs available through multiple avenues, including wireless, hand-held devices, on kiosks, over the intranet, and on personal computers. Today courseware comes on audiotapes and videotapes, CDs, DVDs, through an intranet, and in notebooks. Some programs are downloadable from a website and others are shipped by a warehouse to the learner or learning center. The need to produce training materials in multiple formats has again increased the array of skills required of training professionals. For example, training professionals now have to know how to conduct usability tests to assure user acceptance and confirm that systems are compatible.

THE CELL PHONE COMPANY

Background

The company decided on an aggressive expansion program. It planned to open phone stores in major markets. The plan was to focus on regions, open the stores in major markets in those regions, and then move on to another region.

The Need

Store personnel had to be trained on product features, calling plans, activation of phone service, credit card sales, and more.

The Solution

The company decided to put trainers onsite at each store for the first week; however, it did not want to hire instructors. It decided to find a firm that could act as a sourcing agent and provided instructors experienced in sales and telephone service training. The sourcing firm located independent trainers in each major market. The company arranged for them to come to the corporate headquarters to be trained on how to deliver the content.

Test Learners' Knowledge

The demand for more training has brought with it the expectation that training functions will assess the effectiveness of their programs by specifically testing what people have learned. The software industry has built products that can administer and score paper-based and intranet delivered tests.[1] Training professionals find themselves in the dilemma of how to best leverage this testing software. At a minimum they have to learn how to construct good tests, validate them, conduct criticality analyses, and integrate test results with the LMS and HRIS. The use of tests, in turn, has surfaced other issues such as what information to retain, which people should have access to test results, and what to do when learning falls short of what is expected. Testing requires training professionals to acquire additional skills and build management policies about the use of test results.

Report on Workforce Capability

Running parallel with the increased interest in tests is the increased interest in and adoption of competency studies. Management supports the concept of identifying and assessing people's competencies and matching that to what the organization has identified as being critical to success. Training functions are now expected to link their curriculum to the competencies, add courses to their portfolio that support the competencies, and direct employees to outside resources for additional training, including programs sponsored by colleges and professional associations. Training functions find themselves supporting online reference libraries, course catalogues, and self-assessments. They are expected to rate courses offered by schools, associations, and vendors—requiring them to develop a fair rating method.

CAPABILITY ASSESSMENT

The Need

Senior management asked training to assess the capabilities of all managerial, professional, and sales staff worldwide. Management wanted this information on an annual basis.

The Solution

The training function identified a firm with the capability to develop and administer assessments online. The company contracted with the assessment firm for three years.

Service an Expanding Learning Audience

Another driver of outsourcing is the expansion of the learning audience. Historically, organizations only trained their employees. Today they train customers to the extent that the amount spent on customer training now exceeds that spent for employees.[2] Organizations must also train contractors, independent salesforces, distributors, and technicians who work for product maintenance and repair companies. This wider learner audience is also very dispersed—even worldwide. Some have limited access to technology and communications tools. Some have limited literacy, including in their native language and in the vocabulary of the job. Training is expected to find ways to engage learners throughout the world by making the content meaningful, readable, and accessible. Some organizations are even offering training to the workers' families as a way to build loyalty and help spouses and children be better equipped to address life's issues. A consequence is that the training function must now maintain libraries.

THE ONLINE LIBRARY

The Need

Training was asked to suggest innovative ways to provide training to the workforce with minimal cost. In the past the training function maintained an extensive library of courses. Now it does not have the staff to manage or maintain it.

The Solution

The training department decided to outsource the library. It contracted with a firm that provides an online library containing several hundred titles. Within the first year about 30 percent of the workforce used the library. The company now makes the library available to employees' family members.

Honor Past and Future Commitments

Another challenge training functions face is how to balance past commitments with new client demands. Training functions inherit programs. One answer is to carefully examine the programs and services currently supported to confirm that they are still of value to clients and that the way they are delivered still makes sense. The way programs are delivered may have made sense when they were first launched, but the methods may be inefficient or ineffective to meet current needs. Independent of how effective or efficient they are, the programs still must be maintained. That is, the training function must manage a portfolio of products and programs and has to find ways to keep the content current, track usage, maintain inventories, and replenish out-of-stock materials.

DETERMINE CRITICALITY AND PRIORITY

Training should determine the criticality of clients' demands and decide what the priority should be. Not all needs are equal. Some needs may have to be satisfied before the training function can address others, as one may be a prerequisite to another. For example, to shorten the development and delivery cycle time may require a combination of specialized skills, better work processes, and the latest technology. The challenge is deciding where to begin and deciding whether an external resource can better satisfy the needs.

Figure 2.2, The Demand and Criticality Matrix, illustrates the factors that training functions should consider when deciding what it might possibly outsource based on the criticality of the demand and their ability to deliver. The decision of what is critical should be made in collaboration with clients. The vertical axis is about the training function's capability and capacity to deliver or meet an expectation. The horizontal axis is about how critical the expectation is.

Figure 2.2. The Demand and Criticality Matrix

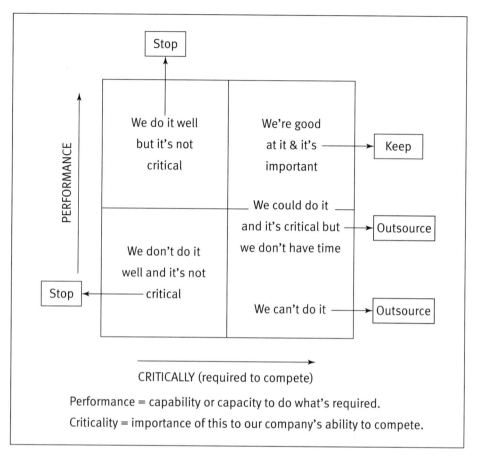

Performance = capability or capacity to do what's required.

Criticality = importance of this to our company's ability to compete.

TOOL 2.1: GUIDELINES FOR IDENTIFYING THE NEED TO OUTSOURCE

Here are some guidelines for identifying the factors that might be driving the need for your training function to either expand its capabilities or outsource. It is in two parts. Part 1 asks you to identify your clients' expectations. Part 2 is designed to help you examine how you are using your current resources, both employees and contractors. Subsequent chapters will build on what you discover.

Part 1: Identify Clients' Expectations and Needs

1. Put together a team from the training function and selected internal clients.

2. Have each member of the team privately list what they see are expectations of the department. To get them started you might list the factors covered in this chapter, such as shorter development cycle time, need to track CEUs, testing, and easier or more rapid access to courseware.

3. If it helps, list the services the department is expected to provide. Opposite each one, note whether it is what you are doing currently, whether just more is expected, or whether something new or different is expected. (See Figure 2.3.)

Figure 2.3. Expectations of Training Worksheet

Expectations of Training	Comments (do now, do more, do different)	Criticality Rating 1–3 *Low --- High*			Ability Rating 1–3 *Low --- High*		
1.							
2.							

4. Have each member of the team privately rate the criticality of the expectation or service using a scale of 1 (low) to 3 (high). For example, a high rating could be due in part to expected product changes or increasing regulation.

5. Have each member of the team privately rate the department's ability to provide those services using a scale of 1 (low) to 3 (high). A low rating could be due to lack of resources or ability. You can take a first pass at this assessment now or wait until you finish Chapter 3, where assessing capacity and capability is discussed in more detail.

6. Take the ratings of the group and identify those expectations that are critical, yet the function was not rated highly, and discuss whether they would be better satisfied if outsourced or whether it is better to invest in improving the department's capability.

Part 2: Examine Current Resource Usage

1. List the training function's current programs and services and the clients of each. Use a table similar to the one shown in Figure 2.4.

Figure 2.4. Evaluation of Current Offerings Worksheet

Current Services or Programs	Client	Resources Required	Rating 1–3 *Low --- High*			Comments
1.						
2.						

Outsourcing Training and Development. Copyright © 2006 by John Wiley & Sons, Inc.
Reproduced by permission of Pfeiffer, an Imprint of Wiley. www.pfeiffer.com

2. Identify the resources required to deliver each program or service. Include trainers (internal and external), facilities, equipment, and technology. Where possible match each resource with a program, service, or client.

3. Poll clients to determine to what degree they value the program or service and ask them to rate each one by its value using a scale of 1 (low) to 3 (high).

4. Identify those services or programs that are rated low and discuss whether they should be eliminated, delivered differently, or outsourced.

5. Identify those services or programs that consume a lot of resources or expensive resources and discuss whether they might be better handled if outsourced.

IMPLICATIONS

The increased reliance on training to assure the capability of the workforce and end users can contribute to a distorted understanding of all that is required for people to perform effectively. Certainly job skills and product knowledge are important, especially since they are constantly changing. However, skills and knowledge alone do not guarantee performance, competitiveness, or acceptance. Other variables play a role, such as clear directions, access to adequate resources, well-designed work processes, and the use of appropriate incentives. Training professionals have an obligation to help management better understand what is required for individual and organizational performance. If they fail to build that appreciation, they risk management having unrealistic expectations and looking for simple solutions. At the same time, training professionals have to step up to the reality that they must continue to broaden their skills and become astute consumers and users of technology and systems.

MISSTEPS AND OVERSIGHTS

A misstep is not involving senior management in the needs assessment process. Outsourcing decisions are frequently driven by senior management's desire to cut costs or shift them from fixed to variable costs by lowering the internal head count. Unfortunately, the training function is often seen as a non-core function that adds cost without providing value. In this situation, outsourcing decisions may have little to do with learning. Also, senior management are rarely the primary clients of the training function, which is why it is so important to involve them in the needs assessment process; otherwise training professionals and their main clients may never understand why the decision was made to outsource, such as it was in response to a merger, acquisition, or new market opportunity.

Another common misstep or oversight is to overlook the importance of confirming exactly what clients require and expect of training. Training runs the risk of over-engineering its training, designing to a level that exceeds the need, or relying on solutions that by themselves are inadequate to fully satisfy clients. Overly designed programs increase the development cycle time and the cost. Similarly, relying on one delivery method or one training solution for all needs may be an inappropriate or ineffective way to meet some needs. Training departments should consider multiple approaches to meeting the needs of clients. This in turn requires them to engage partners whose capabilities are aligned with what clients require and who have the versatility to make use of the most appropriate technologies. Outsourcing firms that bring only one solution or one approach to clients' needs will not be able to effectively meet all needs to build the capability of the workforce nor that of the training function.

Another oversight is the unwillingness to examine the programs and services currently offered. Sometimes organizations outgrow certain programs and how current internal resources are used. If a goal is to increase the capability of the training function, one way is to eliminate programs and services that are no longer required so that internal and external resources can be assigned to programs that are valued.

SUMMARY

In response to the growing demands for more, faster, just-in-time training, training functions should look for partnerships that will

- Give them access to the latest specialized training development and delivery tools and technologies with minimal investment
- Expand the type of delivery options and increase the speed of delivery
- Provide self-service course registration systems and automated testing
- Support the just-in-time training and reporting needs of line managers

WHERE TO LEARN MORE

Here are some resources for learning more about what is required to optimize new learning technologies:

Horton, W., & Horton, K. (2003). *e-Learning tools and technologies*. New York: John Wiley & Sons. This book is very thorough and easy to read. It is an excellent resource for organizations that want to better understand what is required to effectively build web-based and computer-based training.

NOTES

1. Specialized software is available to do testing; for example, QuestionMark, Random Test Generator—Pro, and Survey Tracker. Some authoring systems have built-in testing capability, such as Lectora. See the Horton and Horton book to get a more comprehensive list of products designed to support testing.
2. According to research done by The Exceleration Group in 2003, of the total dollars corporations spend on training activities, 52 percent goes to customer education activities, 42 percent goes toward employee learning activities, and 6 percent goes to training supply chain interests (channel partners and suppliers). See Outsourcing Training, Facts and Figures at www.outsourcingtraining.com.

Figure 3.1. The Engagement Process, Phase 2: Assessing Capacity and Capability

Phase 1: Identifying the Need	Phase 2: Assessing Capacity and Capability	Phase 3: Selecting the Outsourcing Firm	Phase 4: Contracting	Phase 5: Starting Up	Phase 6: Managing the Relationship	Phase 7: Closing Out
Determine client's needs a. shorten cycle times b. deliver more training • regulation • turnover c. provide greater access to training d. test learners' knowledge e. report on workforce capability f. expanding learning audience g. honor past and future commitments Determine criticality and priority	Assess strengths a. credibility and trust b. capacity c. capability d. knowledge and skills e. resources f. work processes g. standards Assess weaknesses Conduct job task analysis a. by role b. by task and skill	Set the baseline Define roles and responsibilities Define the requirements Define the selection criteria Recruit potential outsourcing firms Issue the RFQ Issue the RFP Convene the panel and decide	Prepare the contract Draft master agreement Determine scope of work a. deliverables b. reporting requirements c. problem resolution d. quality and service level e. timeliness and termination Draft addenda Agree on terms and conditions a. Accountability b. Budget c. Fees d. Flexibility e. Quality statement f. Service level statement	Build contract profile Set up governance process Develop management plan and schedule Create communication protocols Develop document standards and controls Agree on deliverable standards Identify intellectual property Create transition plan Create dispute resolution process	Provide oversight Implement the plan and protocols Share expectations and agree on goals Communicate Stay current with needs Measure and report results Celebrate success Improve processes	Notify about termination Transfer intellectual property Return physical property Reconcile financial obligations Terminate clearances, codes Execute final performance review Orient the training function

Chapter 3
Assessing Capacity and Capability

*T*his chapter continues The Engagement Process with a focus on assessing the training function's strengths and weaknesses, as the demands can be so extensive it is impossible to develop sufficient internal capability to do the whole job. After determining the learning needs of the organization, training should examine its own performance and its capability and capacity to satisfy those needs.

ASSESS STRENGTHS

Strengths depend on the collective abilities of the training function as a whole. What attribute is considered a strength will depend on what the organization values, what the training function is expected to deliver, and how effectively and efficiently it can deliver what is needed. Some training functions have few resources, while others have the latest projection and delivery equipment and software; operate attractive facilities capable of supporting web-based training and computer-generated simulations; provide sophisticated training laboratories; and have access to qualified vendors.

THE RETAILER

Background

The retailer has almost 4,000 stores that sell healthcare, cosmetics, household, party, and automotive items. Most of the stores have a pharmacy and a food counter where customers can buy sandwiches, salads, and fountain drinks. The company has experienced significant growth and anticipates that growth to continue. It has more than 150,000 employees, and twelve distribution centers.

Currently there are ninety professionals in the centralized training department, twenty-two support the creation of online courses, training on the use of the intranet, and management of the learning system. The annual training budget will exceed $9 million in the coming year.

The Situation

The training department wants to move to web-based training. It also wants to invest in an LMS to handle registration, tracking, and documentation. In the past it relied on computer-based training. Here are some of the drivers for change in the way training is delivered:

1. More states are requiring retailers to train cashiers in rules related to the selling of alcohol and tobacco products. The training must cover procedures for validating that customers are of legal age. Turnover at the clerk level is about 90 percent annually. Store managers want the training to be on the company's intranet and available at any time.

2. The company is losing millions of dollars annually because cashiers accept expired and damaged coupons. Customer use of store and manufacturers' coupons is expected to increase.

3. There is a national certification for pharmacy technicians. The company pays for employees to prepare and take the national exam. It also pays the continuing education fees required for recertification.

4. Managers of restaurants must be certified in safe food-handling procedures.

5. The company purchased a new inventory management system that will be used by people in distribution and purchasing.

The Need

Training is expected to:

1. Set up the online training to automatically register the cashiers, pharmacists, pharmacy technicians, assistant store managers, and store managers at the time they log onto the system and generate a training record of completion.

2. Create courses for cashiers that average no more than fifteen minutes in length.

3. Develop a distance education curriculum for:

   a. Pharmacy technicians and food handlers that meet the requirements for continuing education units (CEUs), including interactivity, testing, and record retention.

   b. Cashiers on how to process credit card sales, returns, and manufacturers' coupons.

   c. Purchasing and distribution on how to use the new inventory system.

The training function decided to do a careful assessment of its strengths and weaknesses.

Credibility and Trust

An often overlooked asset or strength is the training function's relationships with line managers and its acquired intelligence about the company and its people, products, processes, and culture. This intelligence is not easily replicated by or transferable to an outside resource. Trust and respect that are earned over time can be very powerful. People gain credibility through their actions and their knowledge of the organization's history, products, processes, systems, and customers.

THE RETAILER

The training department has grown along with the company. Over half of the people in training have been with the company for at least twenty years, and they have earned the respect of senior management. The department can show how its approach to training, focusing on learners' on-the-job performance, has contributed to the company's profitability. Over the years, the department has instituted efficient methods and systems for training development and delivery that better meet clients' needs and generate additional savings that further contribute to the company's profitability.

Capacity

Capacity is another measure of strength. It is about how much work a function can handle. Many training departments have capable people, but there are not enough of them to handle the number of projects expected. The function has to decide whether or not to hire, redeploy, contract, or outsource. If the expected volume is variable or excessive for a long period of time, outsourcing may be a solution, especially if the company wants to limit headcount.

THE RETAILER

The training function hired people with education and experience in instructional design, multimedia, and web- and computer-based technologies. The function had the capability to meet the needs in the past; however, the demand is now so great that it decided it needed to draw on the capabilities of an external resource. The plan was to leverage their internal ability to act as liaisons with store operations, distribution, and purchasing. It could also leverage its knowledge of and experience in building web-based training by helping be a sophisticated consumer of services and products. It determined it had the skills to manage projects and external resources.

THE TELECOM COMPANY

Background

The Telecom company, at its peak, had over 9,000 employees of whom thirty-five were in training. During a major economic downturn, the company laid off 6,000 employees, including twenty-five in the training department. The training budget was cut in half. Over the last year, business has begun to pick up. The company has hired 1,000 employees, but is reluctant to hire any more non-production people, including trainers.

The Need

The company has a need to train the new hires and develop and deliver training on new products. With all of the new products expected to be under development and in the marketplace within the next twenty-four months, it estimates it will need about ten instructional designers who are very experienced in developing web-based training.

The Solution

Not wanting to risk having to lay people off in the future, the company decided to locate a firm that could provide five qualified instructional designers of technical training to supplement the five already on staff.

Capability

Capability is a significant measure of strength. Capability involves a lot more than knowledge and skills, as people may know how, but lack the equipment, tools, funds, or facilities. Therefore, capability includes the adequacy, sufficiency, and appropriateness of:

- *Knowledge, skills, and willingness*—having knowledge and skills that are current and relevant and agreeing to dedicate the time and effort necessary to perform the required tasks in ways clients expect

- *Resources*—having access to equipment, tools, facilities, funds, and people

- *Work processes and standards*—having procedures, work methods, and rules that are efficient and do not consume resources that are too costly

Knowledge and Skills

Know-how is based on experience, education, and background. Some training functions hire people from the line organization on the premise their subject-matter expertise will enable them to quickly develop effective training. Others hire people out of education on the premise they bring knowledge of adult learning theory and presentation skills. Still others come out of information technology (IT). Here is a list of possible strengths in terms of knowledge and skills expected of training professionals:

- *Electronic performance support systems (EPSS)*—proficiency in the design and creation of help screens and the embedding of task procedures in work tools
- *e-Learning*—proficiency with designing and developing courses that maximize the appropriate use of multimedia, computer-based, and web-based technologies and tools
- *Facilitation*—proficiency in delivering classroom training, leading groups, and managing meetings
- *Instructional design*—proficiency in needs analysis, learning theory, instrument design, data analysis, courseware design and development, and the evaluation of learning
- *Multimedia*—proficiency in creating video and audio to convey content and demonstrate learning points or provide practice
- *Performance improvement*—proficiency in needs assessment, collaboration, change management, selecting interventions, and developing strategies to improve or support performance
- *Subject-matter expertise*—knowledge of products and work processes that is acquired through education and experience in key jobs in the organization
- *Technical writing*—proficiency in documenting work procedures, product manuals, and software applications
- *Visuals and graphics*—proficiency in storyboarding, graphics, animation, and video production
- *Web-based technologies*—proficiency in using authoring software to create, deliver, and maintain web-based training
- *Website maintenance and development*—proficiency in building and managing websites

---

THE HR CONSULTING FIRM

Background

The firm manages other companies' benefit programs, including their health, retirement, and incentive plans. The firm continues to expand internationally. Currently, it has four customer support centers located in the United States, Europe, the Far East, and South America. The expansion is putting a great deal of strain on the customer support centers, whose employees respond to very technical questions about health insurance, retirement benefits, and other employee benefits. Currently, the customer support personnel have to toggle among four different databases to respond to customers' questions.

The Need

The company decided to replace its current customer database systems with one enterprise-wide system. As a consequence of this decision, training was asked to identify the training needs of the centers. Training identified about two hundred modules that will need to be created. The decision was made to make the training web-based. The six instructional designers on staff were skilled at developing classroom training, not e-learning. Their experience in using multimedia tools was very limited. They estimated their development time at about 140 hours per one hour of delivery, at a cost of $60 per hour of development time. Management asked training to come up with a way to cut the time by two-thirds and the cost in half.

The Solution

The training function decided to outsource the development of the customer support curriculum. They were able to find a firm with sufficient qualified staff to do the work within the timeframe and at one-fourth the cost.

Resources

Companies are finding that they must invest heavily in e-learning hardware, software, and skilled developers if they want to reap the benefits of blended learning solutions. The investment includes learning management systems (LMS), multimedia development tools, web-based technologies, authoring tools, gaming, animation, and graphics software. The problem is that the investment is ongoing, as new tools and technologies are entering the marketplace on a regular basis. Once the physical resources are available, the next step is investing in training's ability to use them. However, it takes time to build proficiency, which is why companies choose to outsource e-learning development and delivery and the administration and maintenance of the LMS.

THE INSURANCE COMPANY

Background

The company has approximately 40,000 full-time employees. Its products, however, are sold through a network of independent agencies. Training is expected to service the learning needs of employees and the agencies' staff, bringing the learning audience to about 100,000 people.

The Situation

Agencies are demanding access to significantly more information about products, pricing, and customers. Management expects training to meet the agencies' needs, as it believes it will build brand loyalty. At the same time, the industry is expecting increasing regulation, requiring more extensive documentation and record-keeping. The current LMS only tracked employee training. Agencies and the company want the LMS to track all training.

The Need

Training is expected to:

- Have an LMS that accommodates the whole learning population and that tracks agencies' compliance with industry and company requirements
- Add testing to all compliance training
- Make agency training available through the company's intranet
- Increase the amount of courseware it produces annually by one-third

The Solution

The company decided to outsource its LMS.

Work Processes

The design and development of training require efficient processes for it to be cost-effective. The processes start with analyses and end with evaluation. Just like other work processes, training should document them and identify ways to eliminate unnecessary steps or those that consume either too many or too costly resources. Outsourcing brings with it additional processes, such as sourcing, contracting, vendor management, negotiations, quality control, and quality assurance.

Standards

Standards can also help make training more effective and control costs. Training functions that set standards or rules for all phases of development and delivery are in a better position to outsource, as standards are effective tools for communicating expectations. They increase the odds that new programs will be compatible with current systems, and they provide contractors with the information they require to deliver a quality product. There are industry standards for CEU credits, course facilitation, and e-learning products (SCORM and AICC), instructional design, performance improvement, and testing.[1] Companies can supplement these industry standards with their own. Tool 3.1 is an example of guidelines for test developers and those who approve tests.

TOOL 3.1: TEST QUALITY CONTROL GUIDELINES

These guidelines are for the people who develop tests and review tests developed by others.

Test Developers

- If you are developing tests, use the checklist below to review your own work, as it is the one the reviewer will use when evaluating your work.
- If you have developed a test, contact your senior manager to find out who should review it.

Test Reviewers

If you are reviewing a test developed by someone else, use the checklist below.

	Y/N	Comments
1. The test being reviewed is for what program?		
2. How many learning objectives are there?		
3. How many questions make up the test?		
4. Is every question linked to an objective?		
5. Overall does the test sample the learning objectives appropriately?		
6. Are the questions at the appropriate level based on the learning objectives?		
Recognition		
Recall		
Comprehension		
Application		
7. Do the questions comply with the guidelines?		
Multiple-choice		
Multiple-response		
Matching		
Fill-in or short answer		

	Y/N	Comments
True/false		
Performance checklist		
8. Are the instructions on how to take the test complete?		
9. Do the instructions follow the guidelines? (See the tools and guidelines available on *Training's* website.)		

Outsourcing Training and Development. Copyright © 2006 by John Wiley & Sons, Inc. Reproduced by permission of Pfeiffer, an Imprint of Wiley. www.pfeiffer.com

ASSESS WEAKNESSES

Weaknesses, like strengths, can be a matter of degree. The number of tasks expected of the training function and the increasing sophistication of training tools and technologies are putting greater demands on trainers than ever before. Training professionals may fall short of what is expected of them due to the quantity of work to be done or a lack of experience doing the new work. The challenge is how to cost-effectively increase capacity and capability.

CONDUCT JOB TASK ANALYSIS

Training functions are learning that the proliferation of tasks and the skills required can only be done through the collaboration of specialists and access to the latest technology. Conducting a job task analysis is a way to understand what is required to do the expected work and in the process identify the training function's strengths and weaknesses. The analysis can look at the roles training plays and the skills required.[2] The results will help determine whether and what to outsource. It can also link tasks and responsibilities to deliverables.

By Role

Except for some of the management roles, all of the other roles can be outsourced. The more common roles training plays are:

- *Customer liaison*—the people responsible for assessing customers' learning needs, advising them on instructional methods and delivery options, coordinating access to subject-matter experts, working with management to assure project teams are established as needed, and either coordinating with or serving as project leaders. They are usually assigned to a specific customer group, such as marketing, call centers, manufacturing or production, accounting, and so forth. This is a major role played by trainers in professional firms that place them in training as a developmental assignment. The training managers leverage their knowledge of the business and their relationships with the line organization to the benefit of the training function.

- *Management*—the people responsible for sourcing, budgeting, scheduling, and selecting and assigning resources.

- *Project leadership*—the people who coordinate the activities of a team assigned to create a set of deliverables. They may be responsible for project budgets, plans, timelines, status reports, and quality assurance. This is another role that organizations use as a developmental assignment. They want project managers who know the needs and constraints of the business and have established relationships with the line organization.

- *Project team members*—specialists who are assigned specific tasks and deliverables, including design, development, production, system integration, and evaluation.

Collectively these roles need to be performed. Only large training functions can afford full-time specialists on staff. More organizations are finding it necessary to outsource many of these roles.

By Task and Skill

This approach is to divide the work into tasks and identify those the training function is capable of performing because it has the skills and resources, compared to those that might be better outsourced. Here are the main tasks expected of a training function:

- *Administration*—The ability to handle all aspects of registration, coordination, scheduling, and documenting training

- *Assessment*—The ability to design and conduct all types of inquiry, including the design of data-gathering instruments, and analyze the results

- *Design*—The ability to design strategies for building the capability of the workforce, including formal training, on-the-job training, mentoring, job aids, and electronic performance support systems

- *Development*—the ability to construct all of the elements required to execute the design strategy, including the writing of course materials and scripts, creating storyboards for media, shooting and editing video, and then integrating these elements into various media

- *Production*—the ability to reproduce the elements and course materials in print and electronic formats so they are available to learners

- *Delivery*—the ability to convey or disseminate courses and course materials, including instructor-led, broadcast, and web-based

- *Implementation*—the ability to prepare the learning audience and other vested parties so they understand the purpose and value of the learning event and are ready to participate

- *Evaluation*—the ability to establish measures and metrics, design and develop measurement tools, including tests, conduct formative and summative evaluations, and analyze the results

THE SUITE OF SKILLS

Background

A company wanted to take advantage of distance learning. However, to do this it had to expand the capabilities of its current training staff, hire people with the required skills, or outsource to individuals or a firm with the desired capabilities. Here is a list of the jobs and skills the company identified it had to gain access to before it could fully realize the benefits of distance learning:

1. *Instructional Designer Developer:* skills in instructional technology and written communication; experience in multimedia design.; and skill in using Flash, Dreamweaver, and ToolBook

2. *Programmer:* experience using multimedia suite development tools or web-based technologies (Director, Dreamweaver, Flash, ASP.NET, and Lectora, for example); experience with ActionScripting, JavaScript, and DHTML; familiarity with the use of XML and other programming languages; and knowledge of VB.NET, database design, and gaming development

3. *Graphic Artist:* working knowledge of multimedia suite development tools or web-based technologies like Adobe PhotoShop, Adobe Illustrator, 3D MAX, Maya, Poser, Macromedia Flash, Freehand, Fireworks, and Dreamweaver; experience with ActionScripting, JavaScript, and XM.

THE ACCOUNTING FIRM

Background

The firm offered accounting and auditing services to business and industry worldwide. It had 70,000 employees, 18,000 in the United States, and offices in seventy countries. The professionals assigned to accounting and auditing had academic degrees and held professional certifications. Personnel in the training function mostly came from the accounting and audit departments. Their roles were liaisons and project managers. There were a few people in training with degrees in instructional design. Training delivery, most of which was classroom, was outsourced.

The Need

Classroom training was becoming too costly, and executive leadership wanted to demonstrate to customers how the firm was being proactive in assuring the competency of its staff. The training function proposed a performance-based curriculum that incorporated testing of knowledge and skills and partnering with the internal audit function to measure how well staff applied the training content on the job. The curriculum would incorporate both classroom and web-based training.

The Solution

After the leaders in the training function did a careful analysis of the skills and abilities required to deliver performance-based instruction, they determined that as a group they lacked sufficient capacity or capability to design, develop, produce, or administer the new curriculum. However, they wanted to leverage their credibility with the professional practices and their project management skills. The training function decided to outsource all web and classroom curriculum and test development. They also determined that they lacked skills in evaluation, but decided to build that capability internally so they would be in a better position to judge the adequacy of the work produced by contractors. The group then developed instructional design and testing standards and made them available to the outsource company.

MANUFACTURER OF HEAVY EQUIPMENT

Background

The manufacturer makes and services large equipment used in the agricultural, construction, mining, and marine industries. Worldwide the company has about 70,000 employees. Its products are sold through two hundred dealerships located around the world.

The Need

Customers complained that the technicians who maintain and service the equipment were not proficient. They claimed that, instead of diagnosing problems, technicians just replaced parts until the equipment ran.

The training function conducted a major job task analysis of the technician's job. It determined that technicians must know the core systems common across all equipment families, such as hydraulics and electronics, and the operations of specific pieces of equipment. The function also determined that, because of the growing international markets for its equipment, it had to find a way to cost-effectively train technicians throughout the world. Instructors were subject-matter experts in specific equipment families or core systems. In the past the instructors developed and delivered the training either at the technicians' work site or at one of the six major learning centers.

Next, the training function examined its ability to develop and deliver the new curriculum. It determined that it lacked the ability internally to quickly develop web-based learning modules. It did have the ability to design the curriculum and it had acquired an LMS to track all learners worldwide. It decided to improve its capability in the area of evaluation, including testing.

The Solution

The training function decided to outsource all of the course design, development, and production. It will also outsource the hosting of the training website that will house all of the modules. It decided to build capability to do evaluation internally so it would be in a better position to evaluate the products developed by the outsourcing firm.

TOOL 3.2: GUIDELINES FOR ASSESSING STRENGTHS

Here are some guidelines designed to help you assess the training function's strengths and decide what services it might want to outsource. The guidelines build on the initial assessment of the training function's capability done in Chapter 2.

1. Put together a team from the training department and selected internal clients.

2. Have the team decide on an approach for assessing the function's strengths and weaknesses. You might want to do it by role or use a table similar to the one in Figure 3.3.

3. Have each member of the team privately determine the collective skill or capability of the people who make up the training function using a scale of 1 to 3 with level 1 being low and level 3 being high.

4. As a group, discuss everyone's ratings and come to consensus.

5. Compare what is expected from Chapter 2 with what the function can deliver with its current capabilities to identify any gaps.

6. Based on current and future demands, identify those tasks or skill sets you want to develop internally or possibly outsource.

Figure 3.2. Task Skill Capability Matrix

Phase/Tasks	Skill Required	Capability Internal or External	
Project Management	Coordinate Schedule Resources Budget Develop Status Reports Coach Team Members		

Assessment	Design and Conduct:
	    Needs Assessments
	    Cause Analyses
	    Training Needs Analyses
	    Job Task Analyses
	    Audience Analyses
	    Criticality Analysis
	Design Data Gathering Instruments:
	    Surveys
	    Interviews
	    Focus Groups
	    Observations
	    Document Searches
	    Production Reports
	Analyze Data		

Design	Develop Strategies for Building Capability
	Create Business Cases
	    Budget
	    Baseline Metrics
	    Feasibility
	Develop Evaluation Method(s)
	    Reaction
	    Learning
	    Application
	    Impact
	Design
	    Curriculum
	    Courses/Instruction
	    E-learning
	    Blended Learning
	    Distance Learning
	    Web-Pages
	    Databases
	    Performance Support Tools and Systems
	    Report Formats		

Figure 3.2. Task Skill Capability Matrix, (Continued)

Phase/Tasks	Skill Required	Capability Internal or External	

Development	Develop Learning Materials
	Develop Job Aids and Performance Support Tools
	Do Technical Writing
	Do Copy Editing
	Develop Storyboards
	Write Scripts
	Produce Video/Audio
	    Cast
	    Film/Record
	    Edit
	Develop Tests
	Do Layouts
	Do Programming
	Create Graphics
	Create Animation
	Integrate Elements into Lessons
	Integrate Lessons into Courses
	Conduct Formative Evaluations for Accuracy
	    Text
	    Graphics
	    Report Layouts
	    Usability Testing
	    Discrimination Testing
	    Report Generation Testing
	Develop End-of-Course Evaluations		

Production	Print, Duplicate, Package Learning Materials		
Implementation	Develop a Communication Strategy Create and Produce Announcements Schedule Participation		
Delivery	Facilitate Meetings Deliver Presentations Deliver Instructional Programs Deliver Web-Casts Administer Computer-Based Training		
Evaluation	Compile/Process Evaluations Score Tests Track Application Correlate Participation Against Key Metrics Present Findings		

Figure 3.2. Task Skill Capability Matrix (Continued)

Phase/Tasks	Skill Required	Capability Internal or External	
Administration	Track and Record Continuing Education Credits Register People for Classes Maintain Website Produce Course Catalogues Schedule Rooms, Laboratories, Media, Schedule Instructors Distribute Materials, Certificates		

Outsourcing Training and Development. Copyright © 2006 by John Wiley & Sons, Inc. Reproduced by permission of Pfeiffer, an Imprint of Wiley. www.pfeiffer.com

IMPLICATIONS

The growing reliance on outsourcing firms might result in a greater recognition and appreciation of training as a discipline, a profession in its own right, especially if vendors can attract and retain qualified designers and developers who can cost-effectively build technology-based training. The vendors will have to invest in the development of their people to stay competitive. The irony is that if more internal practitioners were capable and managed training as a business, they would be less susceptible to economic swings and being outsourced. Unfortunately, there are few requirements for becoming a trainer, course developer, or training manager, despite the work of the professional societies that support the profession, such as ASTD, the International Society for Performance Improvement (ISPI), and the Society for Human Resource Management (SHRM). Perhaps outsourcing will change that. At a minimum, companies that choose to outsource all or part of the training function will have to be knowledgeable consumers to reap the full benefits of their decision.

MISSTEPS AND OVERSIGHTS

The more common misstep or oversight is to trivialize the breadth and depth of skills required of training functions and their potential contribution to the organization. Managers who may never have seen effective and efficient training may assume that the function brings little value and can, therefore, be outsourced with little risk. When this is the case, the decision to outsource can be oversimplified. For example, the decision to eliminate instructor-led training and replace it with e-learning overlooks the increased importance of courses being well-designed. Instructors can save a poorly designed program by adjusting in real time. This is not the case with e-learning.

Instructional design is a discipline that encompasses the whole set of assessment, analysis, design, and evaluation skills. The introduction of e-learning imposes the need to develop proficiency in designing and producing learning that maximizes the appropriate use of a broad array of web-based capabilities. The globalization of organizations and their markets adds the need to build capability in distance learning. Added to these is the need to be intimate with the organization's products, processes, culture, and personnel. Another misstep is the unwillingness to examine how current training resources are assigned.

While decisions about capital expenditures and make-or-buy decisions reflect an assumed life span of years, the training function is constantly on the edge of being out-of-date. Every change in procedures, client orientation, process, and equipment requires updating the organization's information, communication, performance assessment, and so forth. Therefore, turnaround time, accuracy, and user friendliness are the rule in training.

SUMMARY

The process of deciding if and what to outsource begins with a serious examination of what clients require and what the training function can provide. Training professionals have a wide range of backgrounds. Small departments are more likely to operate as generalists than as specialists. Larger departments may have sufficient work to justify hiring and using internal specialists. The goal is to align the capabilities of the training professionals with what is expected. How those capabilities are actualized can be through a combination of internal and external resources.

WHERE TO LEARN MORE

Here are some resources for learning more about what is required to optimize new learning technologies.

Fallon, D., & Brow, S. (2003). *e-Learning standards.* Boca Raton, FL: CRC Press.

Horton, W., & Horton, K. (2003). *e-Learning tools and technologies.* New York: John Wiley & Sons. This book is very thorough and easy to read. It is an excellent resource for organizations that want to better understand what is required to effectively build web-based and computer-based training.

Rosenberg, M. (2001). *e-Learning: Strategies for delivering knowledge in the digital age.* New York: McGraw-Hill .

Rossett, A. (2001). *Beyond the podium: Delivering training to a digital world.* San Francisco, CA: Pfeiffer.

Hale, J. (2004). *Test development workbook.* Downers Grove, IL: Hale Associates.

1. The standards for instructional design and course facilitation are available through the International Board of Standards for Training Performance and Instruction at www.ibstpi.org. The standards for performance improvement are available through the International Society for Performance Improvement at www.ispi.org. The standards for e-learning products are available through ASTD at www.astd.org. The standards for testing, test items, and the training function are available through Hale Associates at www.HaleAssociates.com. SCORM standards are available from the Advanced Distributed Learning site at www.adlnet.org. AICC standards are available from the Aviation Industry CBT Committee at www.aicc.org. Another standard you might find of interest is 17024 on how to qualify people, published by the International Standards Organization (ISO) and the American National Standards Institute (ANSI). They are available through www.ansi.org.

2. The Department of Labor Bureau of Labor Statistics' *Occupational Handbook* includes an extensive description of the various roles and responsibilities required of training professionals. To learn more, check http://bls.gov/oco/ocos021.htm.

Phase 1: Identifying the Need	Phase 2: Assessing Capacity and Capability	Phase 3: Selecting the Outsourcing Firm	Phase 4: Contracting	Phase 5: Starting Up	Phase 6: Managing the Relationship	Phase 7: Closing Out
Determine client's needs	Assess strengths	Set the baseline	Prepare the contract	Build contract profile	Provide oversight	Notify about termination
a. shorten cycle times	a. credibility and trust	Define roles and responsibilities	Draft master agreement	Set up governance process	Implement the plan and protocols	Transfer intellectual property
b. deliver more training	b. capacity	Define the requirements	Determine scope of work	Develop management plan and schedule	Share expectations and agree on goals	Return physical property
• regulation	c. capability	Define the selection criteria	a. deliverables	Create communication protocols	Communicate	Reconcile financial obligations
• turnover	d. knowledge and skills	Recruit potential outsourcing firms	b. reporting requirements	Develop document standards and controls	Stay current with needs	Terminate clearances, codes
c. provide greater access to training	e. resources	Issue the RFQ	c. problem resolution	Agree on deliverable standards	Measure and report results	Execute final performance review
d. test learners' knowledge	f. work processes	Issue the RFP	d. quality and service level	Identify intellectual property	Celebrate success	Orient the training function
e. report on workforce capability	g. standards	Convene the panel and decide	e. timeliness and termination	Create transition plan	Improve processes	
f. expanding learning audience	Assess weaknesses		Draft addenda	Create dispute resolution process		
g. honor past and future commitments	Conduct job task analysis		Agree on terms and conditions			
Determine criticality and priority	a. by role		a. Accountability			
	b. by task and skill		b. Budget			
			c. Fees			
			d. Flexibility			
			e. Quality statement			
			f. Service level statement			

Figure 4.1. The Engagement Process, Phase 3: Selecting the Outsourcing Firm

Chapter 4

Selecting the Outsourcing Firm

*T*his chapter continues with Phase 3 of The Engagement Process, shown in Figure 4.1, and is about selecting an outsourcing firm. This is the phase in which the training function designs its selection process, decides what services it wants to buy, identifies the criteria it will use to select an outsourcing firm, and determines what information it wants to solicit from potential firms.

DEFINITIONS

Here are some definitions of terms frequently used in discussions about selecting outsourcing firms:

- *Proposal* is an offer by an individual or firm to provide goods or services at a specified price for a specific period of time. It is used in the competitive process by which contracts are awarded based on an evaluation of the proposal against stated evaluation criteria. A proposal is a binding offer to perform.

- *Request for proposal (RFP)* is a document that asks individuals and firms to describe how they would satisfy a request for services, the timing, the fee, and the payment terms.[1]

- *Request for qualification (RFQ) or request for information (RFI)* is a document that asks individuals and firms to describe their capabilities.

- *Stakeholders* are representatives from the groups who will be most impacted by the decision to outsource. Depending on the work, they might include IT, finance, HR, managers, or representatives of the learning audience.

The steps in selecting an outsourcing firm to perform all or some of the roles and duties expected of the training function are

- Set the baseline.
- Define roles and responsibilities.

- Define the requirements.
- Define the selection criteria.
- Recruit potential outsourcing firms.
- Issue the RFQ.
- Issue the RFP.
- Convene the panel and decide.

SET THE BASELINE

Before beginning the process of soliciting information from potential outsourcing firms, the training function should set the baseline or define the current state:

- *Determine its fully loaded costs.* The training function cannot determine how much money is saved from outsourcing if it does not know its current fully loaded costs. This includes salaries, benefits, and dedicated facilities and equipment.

- *Map its training processes.* The training function cannot claim that outsourcing is more efficient in terms of cycle time or use of resources if it has not described its processes sufficiently to estimate cycle times or resource consumption.

- *Assess its internal capability and capacity.* This is particularly important if the training function has downsized or anticipates laying people off. The training function should be clear as to what capabilities and capacity it has and wants from a potential outsourcing firm. This will help it determine the selection criteria.

DEFINE ROLES AND RESPONSIBILITIES

Once the baseline is set and the deliverables defined, the next step is to determine the roles and responsibilities of the various people involved in the selection process, including who decides what the requirements are, who writes the RFP, who solicits bids, whose gets to express an opinion, and so forth. Here are the common roles:

- *Contract administrator*—usually someone from purchasing, procurement, finance, or legal who provides technical guidance related to contracting

- *Contract manager*—the person from the training function who will be responsible for oversight of the selection process and the contract

- *Contracting officer*—the person with the authority to enter into contracts on behalf of the organization. This could be the training director or someone from executive management.

- *Outsourcing firm*—an individual or company that has a contract with the organization to provide training services or goods, synonymous with supplier and vendor

- *Panel or evaluation committee*—the group established to evaluate proposals, consisting of key stakeholders, the people whose success or effectiveness depends on the quality and sufficiency of the training services or goods being solicited. The panel should also decide on the process it wants to use to recruit, evaluate, and select an outsourcing firm. It might want to issue an RFQ to first identify firms with the desired capabilities and capacity and then issue an RFP to those firms with the capabilities to do the work to compare costs.

The decision to outsource should be a joint one and may be done under the guidance of purchasing, procurement, finance, or the legal department. The organization should solicit technical advice if the goal is to engage a firm to develop e-learning programs, host a training website, or manage an LMS. This step goes more smoothly when the roles and responsibilities are defined before entering into conversation with an outsourcing firm. Figure 4.2 is an example of the different roles, their responsibilities, and how they collaborate in the outsourcing decision.

DEFINE THE REQUIREMENTS

This is the step where the panel discusses and agrees on what they want to accomplish and on the services they want to outsource. The training function should have determined exactly what it wants from a potential outsourcing firm and the criteria it will use when evaluating a vendor before starting the solicitation process. The requirements and criteria form the basis for the RFQ and RFP.

- *Deliverables*—these are the combined goods and services the training function wants from outsourcing.

- *Goods*—these are the tangible things the organization wants to buy, lease, or somehow gain access to for a period of time. Some examples of goods are curriculum, courses, equipment, libraries, software applications, and processes that already exist. The organization may want to gain access to training technologies, such as authoring programs, proprietary web or computer software, or an LMS.

- *Services*—these are less tangible, as they are about the expertise or capabilities of people and systems. The services people usually provide are consultation, project management, course development, redesign of training processes, management or customization of the LMS, or hosting the website on which courses reside. Some examples of goods and services are shown in Figure 4.3.

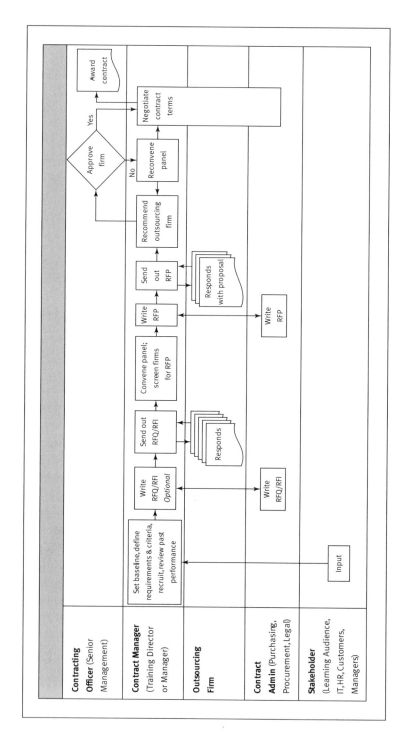

Figure 4.2. The Selection Process

**Figure 4.3. Goods
and Services**

Goods—Courseware	Services—People and System Expertise
Access to an existing library	Access to subject-matter experts
Purchase of a curriculum	Access to skilled developers
Purchase of a LMS or LCMS	Custom instructional design
Purchase of standardized tests	Someone to conduct needs assessments
	Someone to construct or validate tests
	Coaching on evaluation
	Someone to deliver the training

The Relationship

There is an assumption that, when an organization decides to outsource, it just wants to buy access to expertise or acquire goods and services. However, the training function may also want to build its internal expertise or capability and eventually reduce its long-term dependence on the outsourcing firm. If the organization only wants to buy, then the outsourcing firms need only prove they can provide the goods and services. If the organization wants to build internal capability, then the outsourcing firms need to describe their process for transferring their knowledge, processes, or ownership of goods.

Another requirement of the outsourcing relationship is whether or not the outsourcing firm is expected to collaborate with the internal staff to create programs or systems or just do the work itself. If outsourcing firms are expected to collaborate, then the RFQ and RFP should specify how that collaboration is done, the roles and responsibilities of both groups, how and who provides direction or oversight, what standards to use, and how problems will be resolved.

MANUFACTURER OF HEAVY EQUIPMENT

The manufacturer decided to outsource all curriculum development. The manufacturer wanted the outsourcing firm to develop internal staff's ability to do task analyses and develop web-based courses. The outsourcing firm successfully trained the manufacturer's personnel in how to do task analysis because they collaborated while the work was done at the manufacturer's site. It was less effective on transferring skills to develop web-based courses, as that work was done at the outsourcing firm's site more than three hundred miles away.

Another service the manufacturer outsourced was the development of a worldwide certification program for technicians and instructors. The manufacturer wanted the consultant to build the training function's expertise in creating all of the elements required for a certification program, including test construction and validation, standards, processes for appeals and exemptions, and so forth. This was easier to achieve because the consultant worked at the manufacturer's site and had documented all of the processes and procedures used to create a certification.

TOOL 4.1: GUIDELINES FOR DEFINING THE SELECTION PROCESS

Here are some guidelines for helping you begin the process of selecting individuals or firms to outsource some or parts of your training function.

1. Define your contracting process. You might want to create a flow chart like the one shown in the tool below.

2. Define the roles and responsibilities of the various parties who might participate in the decision.

3. Decide what you want from an external resource. You might find it helpful to chart the deliverables on a form similar to the one below.

Goods—Courseware	Services—People and System Expertise

DEFINE THE SELECTION CRITERIA

The next step is to decide on the criteria that will be used to compare outsourcing firms and determine whether they can satisfy the requirements.[2] The performance criteria can be grouped under three major categories, which will be explained further in the sections that follow:

1. Capability measures
   a. *Content expertise*—expectations about having industry, organization, product, system, or process knowledge and experience.
   b. *Discipline or process expertise*—expectations about being proficient in their discipline, such as instructional design, facilitation, project management, system integration, and the creation of web-based learning materials.
   c. *Technological capability*—this includes experience and expertise in the use, creation, and integration of multimedia, web and computer-based learning programs, classroom training, and electronic performance support systems.
2. Capacity—about the ability to supply a sufficient number of resources with the expertise required to satisfy the terms of the contract.
3. Special requirements—these might include restrictions or special demands on sub-outsourcing firms or the outsourcing firm's personnel. It should include the vendor's process for disaster recovery should there be a failure in a data base.

Capability

Capability is the collective expertise, experience, and resources that the external resource can offer that would be of value to the organization. People's capabilities are usually measured in terms of education, specialized expertise, experience, certifications, and knowledge of the organization or its industry. If the organization is interested in the capability of equipment or systems, then the measures might be compatibility with the HRIS system, speed, or capacity. If the requirements include processes, the measures might be cycle time, efficiency, or rigor.

Content Expertise. This includes the outsourcing firm's knowledge of the subject, the organization's products, processes, and industry. The questions to ask might include:

- What is the outsourcing firm's specific capability? Does it bring content knowledge?
- How recent is the knowledge or expertise? Is it dated?

- Does it plan to hire the organization's training personnel to leverage their knowledge of the company's people, products, and systems?
- Does the outsourcing firm's experience include working with an organization's customers, supply chain partners, distributors, or trade association?

Discipline or Process Expertise. This includes education and experience in instructional design, facilitation, programming, and the like. The questions to ask might include:

- Does the outsource firm have instructional design and development expertise? Where did it gain this expertise?
- How deep is the capability? How many people possess the knowledge, experience, or expertise required to do the work of the training function?
- How diverse is the experience? Was it gained through one engagement or has it been tested in numerous environments or situations close to what the organization is experiencing?
- How does the outsourcing firm stay current? What is its commitment to keeping its people up-to-date on the content and the technology?

Technological Capability. This includes the outsourcing firm's expertise in creating web-based and computer-based training, customizing LMS, and so forth. The questions to ask might be

- What is the outsourcing firm's technological capability? What specific technology does it use? Does it have experience developing learning materials in an electronic format that can interface with the organization's systems? Is the outsourcing firm's technology compatible with the organization's?
- Is its strength in the use of learning technologies?
- Does the outsourcing firm rely on its own proprietary technology that locks its customers into its systems? Is it proficient in the use of technologies in the public domain?
- How many different specialists (programmers, graphic artists, gaming, for example) does the outsourcing firm have on staff or access to?
- How does the outsourcing firm identify other specialists if needed?

Special Requirements. This is about the outsourcing firm's way of doing business. Here are some questions:

- What is the outsourcing firm's business model? Does it have full-time employees? Does it rely on subcontractors? What is the outsourcing firm's philosophy toward developing its customers and what is its process for doing so?

- Are the vendor's people full-time, part-time, or subcontractors? Are they on staff now or will they be hired or contracted once the contract is awarded? What countries are they authorized to do work in?

- What is the outsourcing firm's project management capability? Is the project manager full-time and will he or she be fully dedicated to this project?

- Is the outsourcing firm capable of generating the required reports, such as staffing level, project status updates, test scores and analyses, and number of CEUs met?

- Is the outsourcing firm expected to have a performance bond? A performance bond requires vendors to guarantee the quality of their goods and services. Bonds are usually part of a risk management policy.

Capacity

This is about how much work the outsourcing firm can handle and how many resources it can dedicate to doing the organization's work. The external resource may have capable people, but they may be partially or fully committed to other customers. The organization may want to require a minimum number and type of dedicated resources. The questions to ask include:

- How many people does the outsourcing firm have?

- How many customers is it currently serving?

- Can the outsourcing firm recruit people with the required abilities to do the job if necessary?

- What is the outsourcing firm's process for orienting new employees or sub-outsourcing firms?

- Does the outsourcing firm have the capacity to invest in its people and technology?

THE MIDWEST COMPANY

The company wanted:

- A large outsourcing firm that could do everything from creating to testing of computer- and web-based programs

- The outsourcing firm's leadership to be business smart not just relationship people

- The outsourcing firm to learn the firm's purchasing, decision-making, and buying processes
- The outsourcing firm to have a plan and a protocol for interfacing with the firm's L&D managers and subject-matter experts
- The outsourcing firm's leadership to be accessible for updates and available to work on any problems that arose
- The outsourcing firm's designers and developers to understand and comply with the Midwest company's platform and technology
- The outsourcing firm's designers and developers to have expertise in instructional design and be willing and able to collaborate with the IT department, because IT had internal rules that have to be met
- The outsourcing firm to not by-pass L&D, unless previously agreed to, because L&D wants to be the primary point of contact and coordinator of services
- The outsourcing firm to have the capacity in terms of talent to deliver learning programs within the expected time frame

The panel did not care where the outsourcing firm or its developers were located.

Special Requirements

There may be special requirements of the outsourcing firm that are unique to the nature of the work or the business model of the organization. For example, the training function may want outsourcing firms who:

- Are willing to commit to using local resources
- Are willing to commit to using disadvantaged business enterprises, like women and minority-owned companies
- Are willing to hire the company's former employees or those who are expected to be laid off
- Can get security clearances for their personnel and subcontractors
- Can travel internationally
- Are proficient in one or more languages
- Have certificates of insurance and safety permits
- Can work in an environment where there is controlled access to data or facilities
- Are located close enough to have ready access to subject-matter experts or internal team members
- Have subject-matter expertise

- Have industry experience
- Use software that is in the public domain, such as Dreamweaver, Flash, or Lectora, instead of proprietary software
- Have documented processes for design, development, evaluation, and project coordination
- Have experience working collaboratively with internal resources
- Are established businesses that are financially stable
- Have a disaster recovery plan in place in case of a system failure that puts courseware, content, test results, or records of learning at risk

THE RETAILER

The retailer has very capable instructional designers and developers on staff with experience developing web-based programs. It did not have enough for the volume of work to be done. The team selected to evaluate outsourcing firms to develop courseware for the stores decided on the following criteria and cautions. The outsourcing firm had to:

- Have experience working closely with an inside team. Caution if the outsourcing firm's experience was limited to doing the work by itself.
- Have a deep level of knowledge of instructional design (ID) and a sufficient number of qualified people to do instructional design and development. Caution if the outsourcing firm is primarily loaded with sales and marketing staff.
- Have a good retention record, whether the developers were on staff or sub-outsourcing firms. Continuity of personnel is essential to meet deadlines. Caution if the outsourcing firm does not have a good retention record.
- Use an instructional systems design process consistent with professionally recognized standards. Caution if the firm is just into developing snazzy-looking web pages and templates.
- Have measured the impact of its work with other clients. Caution if it has little history of designing an evaluation strategy that incorporates measures that are meaningful to clients.
- Be able to meet frequently with subject-matter experts, internal team members, and IT. Caution if we're paying travel expenses here, as that adds extra cost and possible slippage of the schedule due to problems communicating and coordinating our work.
- Agree to spend sufficient time onsite working with IT to confirm its programs run on our system and hardware network, not just theirs. Caution if it is unwilling to dedicate the time to assure the program runs on our system.

SELECTION CRITERIA

The Telecom Company training function met with representatives from manufacturing and operations. Together they identified and weighted in terms of importance what they expected from an outsourcing firm. The factors they thought most important were

- Degrees in instructional design
- Experience developing multimedia courseware on technical subjects for the telecom industry

The accounting firm ranked its expectations as follows:

- Experience in the industry
- Education in instructional design
- Experience developing performance-based training
- Experience developing web- and classroom-delivered training
- Demonstrated skills in diplomacy
- Being local

The airport ranked their expectation as follows:

- Experience in performance improvement
- Proof of past performance doing similar work
- Commitment to using local disadvantaged business enterprises (LDBE) as sub-outsourcing firms

---

TOOL 4.2: GUIDELINES FOR SETTING SELECTION CRITERIA

Here are some guidelines for helping you begin the process of selecting individuals or firms to outsource some or parts of your training function.

1. Define your selection criteria. You might find the list below helpful.

   Capability

   Capacity

   Special

   Other:

---

2. Be sure to consider any special requirements, such as those listed next.

Requirements	Y/N	Comments
• Use local resources		
• Use disadvantaged business enterprises, such as women and minority-owned companies		
What percentage?		
• Hire former employees		
• Security clearances		
• Travel internationally		
• Proficient in one or more languages		
Which languages?		
• Certificates of insurance and safety permits		
• Work in controlled access to data or facilities		
• Located locally		
• Subject-matter expertise		
• Industry experience		
• Use software that is in the public domain		
• Use proprietary software		
• Have documented processes for design, development, evaluation, and project coordination		
• Experience working collaboratively with internal resources		
• Established businesses that are financially stable		
• Disaster recovery plan in place		

RECRUIT POTENTIAL OUTSOURCING FIRMS

Recruitment is about asking outsourcing firms to respond rather than publishing the RFQ or RFP on the website and hoping the right person sees it. One way is to ask vendors one has done work with in the past. If the training function is in a contractual relationship with a firm, there is usually a time limit. Independent of how effective or successful the relationship is, the training function is usually required to initiate a competitive bid process. When this happens, the training function asks the outsourcing firms with whom it has worked in the past to respond to a request for qualification (RFQ) or a request for proposal (RFP). The training function is exercising due diligence when it asks outsourcing firms to reconfirm their capability and that their terms are competitive.

Another way to recruit is to attend national and international conferences and tradeshows, as established outsourcing firms tend to exhibit there and sometimes give presentations. The leaders of the training function can also network with directors and managers from other organizations, perhaps not in the same industry, but with similar challenges. However, before recruiting, it is best to be clear about what the training function wants from the relationship.

THE RETAILER

The training function has met the demand for courses for the stores in the past, but the increase in the number of programs, the requirements for testing and record retention, and the need to manage all aspects of the intranet and its servers was more than current staff could handle. A discussion ensured about outsourcing as a solution. The objective was to decide whether outsourcing would be a viable long-term solution, and if so, what exactly to outsource. The group consisted of:

- Director of Learning and Development (L&D)
- Manager of L&D Systems Training
- Manager of Employee Relations
- Manager of Leadership Development

The group met to identify all of the tasks the training function was expected to do and assess the department's ability to perform those tasks. What the group discovered was that the department was very capable, but lacked the capacity to develop all the web-based training required.

The training function attended conventions and expos regularly and had identified the firms it wanted to ask to respond. It decided to start by sending the outsourcing firms an RFQ and, based on their responses, follow up with an RFP.

ISSUE THE RFQ

A request of qualification or request for information can help screen out outsourcing firms that lack the minimum capability or capacity for the job. The RFQ, for example, might ask outsourcing firms to explain their industry experience, describe their work processes, document their standards, and explain the qualifications of their people. It might ask for financial information and performance bonds and a commitment to fulfilling the terms of the contract and producing work of sufficient quality. The RFQ may also ask outsourcing firms to provide a statement of intent and a statement of commitment. Tool 4.3 outlines the information that might be asked for in an RFQ.

TOOL 4.3: GUIDELINES FOR THE RECRUITMENT PROCESS

Work with your selection team.

1. Decide how you will identify outsourcing firms. You might place ads in professional and trade journals, recruit outsourcing firms you have worked with in the past, or call colleagues and professional associations for recommendations.

2. Decide how you will ask outsourcing firms to respond. Do you want to start with an RFQ or do you want an RFP? An RFP requires you to be more specific in your request. You might want to use the RFQ template below as a guide.

3. Partner with your legal and procurement departments to develop the RFQ and RFP.

RFQ Template

The RFQ or RFI should contain the following information:

1. Instructions for responding to the RFQ

   Rules about who may or may not be contacted if the outsourcing firm has questions

   Contact information for the person who can be contacted with questions

2. A general description of the type of contract and the goods and services being sought

3. A description of the type of information the organization wants about the outsourcing firm

A general description of the outsourcing firm's experience

A description of the outsourcing firm's past performance doing similar work, in terms of:

- Cost reduction

- Quality of performance

- Compliance with schedules

- Stability of the workforce

A description of the outsourcing firm's five most recent contracts doing work of similar size and complexity

- Client's contact information

- Detailed description of the work performed for one of the five

Description of the experience and qualifications of the outsourcing firm's personnel projected to do the work described in this RFQ

- Employment status—employees or sub-outsourcing firms

- Name, title, resume, education, and experience of the people who would be assigned to do the work

- Name, title, resume, education, and experience of the person who will be the project manager and his or her employment status

4. Any required certifications

5. A statement of intent

6. A statement of commitment

Statement of Intent. The statement of intent asks the outsourcing firm what part of the contract it is responding to. The RFQ may list a whole series of services; however, the outsourcing firm may only want to compete for a selected number of them.

Statement of Commitment. The RFQ may ask the outsourcing firm to commit to specific terms. For example, the RFQ might stipulate that at least 25 percent of the contract must be done by a disadvantaged business enterprise or by outsourcing firms within one hundred miles of the organization's headquarters. What follows is an excerpt from an RFQ.

THE GENERAL STATEMENT OF WORK

The organization plans to retain professional services for an open end, call order type* contract in support of developing a strategic human resource function that adds value to its performance through effective management of human capital. The assistance may include and is not limited to ongoing research to evaluate the operations of the human resource function and the integration of human resource information systems and activities to support the organization's changing business strategies and work flow.

The organization may award multiple contracts for a one-year duration with options for two one-year extensions. A minimum of one call order will be issued by each contract. Each firm, team, or joint venture shall have in-house or subcontracting capabilities to handle the following:

1. Leadership/Management Development—assistance in creating a model that provides all levels the opportunity to develop and refine strong skills for a performance based environment.

2. Performance Management Support and Facilitation—expertise in providing assistance to the organization's managers and workgroups to maintain or improve their performance in a constantly changing environment. This includes identifying and improving critical business and work processes.

3. Diversity Awareness and Training Program Support—assistance in developing programs aimed at creating a culture that takes deliberate actions to increase individual awareness of all dimensions of diversity, to tap into and maximize the talent and productivity of all employees, and to maintain compliance with applicable laws, regulations, and policies.

4. Employment Program Support—assistance in assessing the current selection system for a strategic perspective to maintain the ability to hire, orient, and retain a quality, diverse workforce. It may include implementing workplace and workforce transitions, skill assessments, succession planning, and outplacement services.

A response to this RFQ must include:

- A statement of commitment to meeting the 25 percent Local Disadvantage Business Enterprise (LDBE) participation requirement
- A statement of intent as to what parts of the request the outsourcing firm is responding to

---

*An open-end contract does not cite specific deliverables or time frame. The expression "call order" is analogous to a work order or addendum. During the term of the contract the organization promises to issue at least one call order a year for specific services.

- Identification of the LDBE firm(s) and their tasks
- Documentation of LDBE certification
- Statement of qualifications
  Experience
  Past performance
- Experience and qualification of personnel

ISSUE THE RFP

The request for proposal asks more specific information related to the need or requirements. It asks outsourcing firms to describe their services and their deliverables, how they would satisfy the need, and to specify their fees and payment terms. The RFP includes the deadline for submitting proposals, rules for submitting questions, and the criteria that the panel will use to the evaluate proposals. The rules for submitting questions might include an email address that outsourcing firms can use and the deadline. The RFP may contain other information that will help potential outsourcing firms focus their responses; for example, it should contain the following:

- *Background or needs*—the background statement usually describes why the organization is seeking assistance and the problem or need the organization wants to solve or satisfy.

- *Budget range*—a budget range prevents outsourcing firms from submitting proposals that will be discarded because they are too expensive or too cheap to be believable.

- *Criteria*—the criteria helps outsourcing firms decide whether they are at all competitive. The criteria should address capability, capacity, quality, budget breakdown, and any special requirements.

- *Ownership of the materials*—the RFP might ask the outsourcing firm to specify what exactly the organization will own if given the contract. Most work done under a contract is considered work for hire, and the products of the work are owned by the employing organization. However, the graphic, animation, video, audio, photographs, software, systems, and technologies used to produce the work may not be covered under the work-for-hire provision. If equipment, software, and so forth are not available in the marketplace, but are proprietary to the outsourcing firm, this needs to be stipulated in the outsourcing firm's proposal.

nance bond—the RFP should state whether or not the outsourcing
required to have a performance bond, and if so, for how much.

—the RFP might ask the outsourcing firm to specify what stan-
uses to assure the quality of its goods or services.

or service level—the RFP might ask the outsourcing firm for a
ment to provide adequate staffing with qualified people.

THE MIDWEST COMPANY

t company has historically outsourced development and production
naterials to small and mid-size training companies. The company did
1-house. The company decided that it wanted to outsource all of its
;n and development because it had to reduce headcount and the re-
'f could no longer keep up with the demand or the advances in tech-
remaining staff would become project managers. The company
outsource to three different types of outsourcing firms:

ales and leadership curriculum, it decided to license off-the-shelf
:s and contract with a firm that only does sales and leadership
 to customize the exercises to reflect the company's products and
n.

:t with a sourcing agency to handle all small contracts going to
utsourcing firms. It did not want anyone in the company to bypass
rcing firm, and it did not want outsourcing firms to contact a man-
her than the director of learning and development (L&D).

one large training company to do the design and development of all
hnical courses that will be delivered electronically.

The firm decided to start by issuing an RFQ and then the RFP. It decided to
only invite large training companies that were businesses, have a profit-and-loss
statement, a web presence, multiple clients, and can show a profit.

The team sent the RFQ to the outsourcing firms it had outsourced development to in the past. It also contacted some of the larger outsourcing firms they
had heard about from their professional colleagues.

The selection team was made up of managers in L&D and representatives
from the internal client organization. Together they pre-screened outsourcing
firms based on their responses to an RFQ. When they weeded the list down to
two possible outsourcing firms, they asked people from procurement and legal
to join them.

TOOL 4.4: GUIDELINES FOR SUBMITTING THE RFP

The following guidelines are intended to help you develop the RFP so it solicits adequate information for the panel to make an informed decision:

1. Meet with the panel. Review the information that should be included in the RFQ. Identify what additional information is desired from vendors.

2. Consider the information shown in the template.

RFP Template

Background statement
Budget range

Selection Criteria

Ownership of the materials
Performance bond or insurance
Quality requirements
Staffing or service level commitment
Other

CONVENE THE PANEL AND DECIDE

Once outsourcing firms have submitted their responses to the RFQ and RFP, the panel should review each submission independently. The members should use criteria they established before sending out the RFQ or RFP to evaluate them.

TOOL 4.5: GUIDELINES FOR SELECTING AN OUTSOURCING FIRM

Here are some guidelines for helping you begin the process of selecting individuals or firms to outsource some or parts of your training function. The panel might use a checklist like the one shown in Figure 4.4 to evaluate outsourcing firms.

Figure 4.4. Selection Criteria Checklist

Capability
Capacity
Special
Other:

The panel should agree on the capability and then privately rate each proposal independently. Next, the panel members should share their rankings, discuss them, and then come to an agreement on which outsourcing firm best meets the organization's needs.

IMPLICATIONS

One of the challenges training functions have is matching the outsourcing firm's capabilities with what they require. If the training function enters into a relationship with a firm with far more capability than it requires, it runs the risk of losing access to the most capable people when the outsourcing firm enters into a larger contract with someone else. At the same time, the training function's requirements may grow. In this case it should want a partner willing and capable of growing as well. The training function may find it necessary to invest in the outsourcing firm, enabling it to acquire more talent or the latest technology.

MISSTEPS AND OVERSIGHTS

Here are some of the more common oversights that organizations make. They fail to establish a baseline against which they can eventually determine the effectiveness of their outsourcing decision. They especially fail to calculate the fully loaded training costs. Organizations fail to define or put in place a formal process for contracting for services. They do not take the time to fully define what metrics they will use to compare outsourcing firms or how they intend to measure the success of the outsourcing relationship. They do not involve key stakeholders in the process of determining the requirements or criteria for selecting an outsourcing firm.

SUMMARY

Outsourcing firms believe organizations could do more work up-front to define their requirements and their selection criteria. They believe having a clear understanding of their needs and criteria provides a stronger foundation for the relationship. Outsourcing firms can offer guidance on how to improve the recruiting and selection process. They, too, have criteria. They want to work with organizations that are experienced in partnering with external resources.

WHERE TO LEARN MORE

You may want to consider checking out Ray Svenson's *Strategic Planning Workbook,* available through Amazon.com.

Achieving a Leadership Role for Training describes how the training function can apply the Baldrige quality criteria and the ISO 9000 standards to its own operations. It has examples of training's processes and how they might be documented and improved. The book is available through Hale Associates at Haleassoci@aol.com.

NOTES

1. If the organization has multiple locations in different countries, the affiliate or division that will most benefit from the work should develop the RFP for the specific goods or services. There are tax reasons why the local affiliate or division should be the contracting party.

2. It might be helpful to meet with someone in finance to find out whether your organization has a financial model that could be used to help decide what services to outsource. For example, it might have guidelines for making build versus buy decisions.

Phase 1: Identifying the Need	Phase 2: Assessing Capacity and Capability	Phase 3: Selecting the Outsourcing Firm	Phase 4: Contracting	Phase 5: Starting Up	Phase 6: Managing the Relationship	Phase 7: Closing Out
Determine client's needs	Assess strengths	Set the baseline	Prepare the contract	Build contract profile	Provide oversight	Notify about termination
a. shorten cycle times	a. credibility and trust	Define roles and responsibilities	Draft master agreement	Set up governance process	Implement the plan and protocols	Transfer intellectual property
b. deliver more training	b. capacity	Define the requirements	Determine scope of work	Develop management plan and schedule	Share expectations and agree on goals	Return physical property
• regulation	c. capability	Define the selection criteria	a. deliverables	Create communication protocols	Communicate	Reconcile financial obligations
• turnover	d. knowledge and skills	Recruit potential outsourcing firms	b. reporting requirements	Develop document standards and controls	Stay current with needs	Terminate clearances, codes
c. provide greater access to training	e. resources	Issue the RFQ	c. problem resolution	Agree on deliverable standards	Measure and report results	Execute final performance review
d. test learners' knowledge	f. work processes	Issue the RFP	d. quality and service level	Identify intellectual property	Celebrate success	Orient the training function
e. report on workforce capability	g. standards	Convene the panel and decide	e. timeliness and termination	Create transition plan	Improve processes	
f. expanding learning audience	Assess weaknesses		Draft addenda	Create dispute resolution process		
g. honor past and future commitments	Conduct job task analysis		Agree on terms and conditions			
Determine criticality and priority	a. by role		a. Accountability			
	b. by task and skill		b. Budget			
			c. Fees			
			d. Flexibility			
			e. Quality statement			
			f. Service level statement			

Figure 5.1. The Engagement Process, Phase 4: Contracting

Chapter 5

Contracting

*T*he focus of this chapter is on Phase 4 of The Engagement Process, shown in Figure 5.1. This is the phase when the training function works with its legal, procurement, and finance departments and the outsourcing firm to develop the contract and any required addenda. The people who draft the contract require information from the training function to draft language that supports the intent of the agreement.

Creating the contract is a process, as shown in Figure 5.2, that involves the legal and procurement departments, sometimes risk management and internal audit, the training function, and the outsourcing firm. The process goes more smoothly when all of the parties understand their role and what goes into creating a contract. It is also helpful when professionals in training understand the common terms used it contracting.

DEFINITIONS

There are agreed-on conventions about how contracts are structured and what language goes where. To better understand those conventions, here are some definitions of terms frequently used in discussions about contracting:

- *Contract* is a mutually binding legal document between the organization and an outsourcing firm to obtain training services or goods under specified terms and conditions. A purchase order when accepted by an outsourcing firm is a type of contract.

- *Master, umbrella, or general services agreement* is that part of a contract that contains the general terms and conditions that apply to all of the work being requested of the outsourcing firm.

- *Addendum,* sometimes called a "work order," is a supplement to the master agreement. It contains provisions for specific goods and services to be provided and is, therefore, more detailed. An example might be a

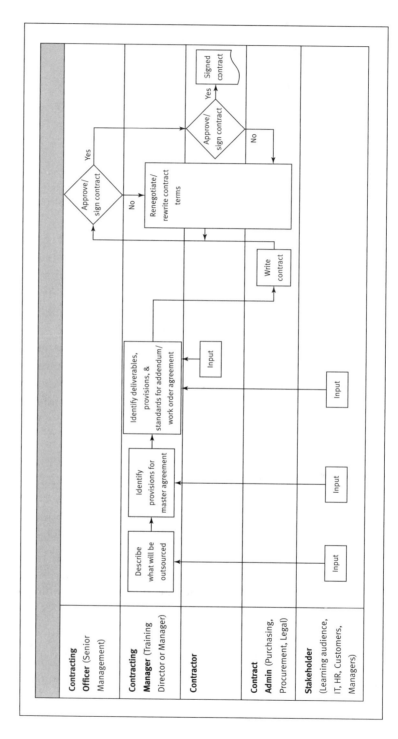

Figure 5.2. The Contracting Process

request for a specific suite of courses beginning with the task analysis and ending with production. The addendum contains terms and conditions that are specific to the request, such as fees and payment terms.

- *Statement of work* is a document that can be prepared by either the organization or the outsourcing firm. When prepared by the outsourcing firm it is in connection with an addendum for a specific project, deliverable, or service. The outsourcing firm describes how it would provide specific services or goods, within what time frame, and at what cost.

PREPARE THE CONTRACT

It is not uncommon for an organization and outsourcing firm to enter into a contract in which the work to be performed is referred to in general terms, such as "manage the training function" or "develop curricula." When this is the case, the organization prepares a master agreement and then adds to it addenda for specific services or goods. Figure 5.3 shows the main parts of a contract and their relationship.

Figure 5.3. Hierarchy of Contract Elements

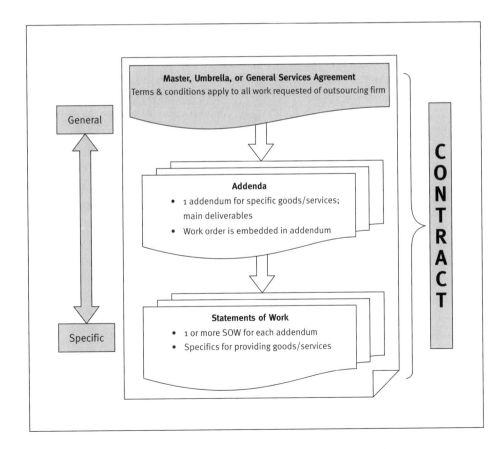

DRAFT MASTER AGREEMENT

The purpose of the master agreement is to get the outsourcing firm into the accounts payable system, be assigned a number, and agree on the basic contract terms that will govern the parties' relationship. The master agreement usually contains a general description of the goods and services being requested and the general provisions. The master agreement rarely contains language about a specific project or program. For example, a request for services in the master agreement might read:

> Employment Program Support—assistance in assessing the current selection system from a strategic perspective to maintain the ability to hire, orient, and retain a quality, diverse workforce. It may include implementing workplace and workforce transitions. Skill assessments, succession planning, and outplacement services may be required.

The master agreement contains the general provisions of the overall contractual relationship. These are the terms and conditions that apply to all deliverables specified in addenda. They are the basic rules of engagement. The provisions that are most frequently included are

- *Confidentiality.* This provision requires the outsourcing firm to agree to honor or maintain the confidentiality of the organization's intellectual property and to not disclose proprietary information and documents, processes, and products.

- *Efficacy of Operations.* This provision requires the outsourcing firm to agree to conduct work in an efficient manner, use resources appropriately, and continuously improve its processes. This provision may require the outsourcing firm to have documented work protocols, review procedures, and a problem resolution process.

- *Exit Clause.* This provision specifies how much notice each party must give the other before ending the master agreement, which should specify under what circumstances either party might end the master agreement and whether or not a reason is required, how much notice is required, and to whom, and how the notice should be sent. How much notice to give depends on the complexity of the relationship and how difficult it will be to transfer property and assignments.

- *Financial Stability.* This provision requires the outsourcing firm to agree to give evidence of financial stability and perhaps even disclose its financial situation and any threats to its solvency. The provision may include a clause about exempting the organization from certain financial liabilities to the outsourcing firm, such as employment taxes and employee benefits. The outsourcing firm may be asked to submit a Dun and Bradstreet report, a credit rating, or annual financial statements.

- *Governance.* This provision requires the outsourcing firm to agree to honor the governance procedure established for the duration of the master agreement.

- *Indemnification Clause.* This provision requires the outsourcing firm to hold the organization harmless if the organization is sued for actions of the outsourcing firm. The organization, in turn, agrees to hold the outsourcing firm harmless should it be sued for actions of the organization.

- *Liability Limitation.* This provision establishes the limitations on the outsourcing firm's liability for consequential damages, such as lost profits and loss of goodwill. For example, the outsourcing firm's liability may be limited to an amount equal to the fees earned by the outsourcing firm or two times that amount. This provision most likely would not apply to intentional acts.

- *Ownership of the Materials.* This provision specifies who owns the materials created by the outsourcing firm for the organization. Sometimes the master agreement calls for the outsourcing firm to create intellectual property. When this is the case, ownership should be clearly established in the master agreement. Questions about ownership go beyond the deliverables. Ownership applies to all of the elements used or discovered during the creation of courseware, such as the design, and any data collected during the term of the contract. It includes all of the elements used in the creation of the learning materials, such as photographs, graphics, illustrations, animation, games, tests, narratives, practice exercises, and more. It also includes the software and systems used in the process. Unfortunately, frequently organizations discover they own the finished product but do not own or have access to the technology, systems, software, devices, or expertise required to maintain or update it. They find they have to pay royalty and licensing fees to use the courseware. The provision related to ownership should also address copyright laws. The outsourcing firm should be expected to assure it has not violated any copyright laws while developing the courseware. If content is reused from another source, then the outsourcing firm should obtain permission in writing to use it. However, the organization's legal department may prefer to obtain any required permissions.

DEFINE SCOPE OF WORK

What will be provided by whom and by when? This and other questions must be agreed to in the contract. However, it is almost impossible to identify all of the elements that will be created, acquired, leased, and used in the creation of learning courseware; therefore the training function should ask the outsourcing firm a series of questions about reusing or modifying the courseware developed as part of the contract. The questions to the outsourcing firm might include:

- Can we use or modify the courseware after the contract expires without permission or additional fees?
- What tools will be required to modify or revise the courseware, and are they in the public domain?
- Will we be restricted to using the outsourcing firm's software or systems?
- Will you provide a comprehensive list of all of the elements used to create the courseware and specify its source and whether it is licensed or owned by the training function, and if not, what the source is and whether fees or royalties are required to reuse them?
- Will you use software in the public domain?
- How will you distinguish the work you create for us from similar work created for other clients? Will you use a file naming scheme, domains of a server, or some other method?

Reporting Requirements

This provision is about the outsourcing firm's obligation to submit special reports in a timely fashion. The reports might be about

- The courseware being created, such as design documents, content outlines, learning objectives, and user test results
- Management of the project, such as activity reports, and staffing level for certain parts of a project
- Safety or how the outsourcing firm plans to comply with all laws and regulations pertaining to the work and operate in a manner that does not put people, property, confidential information, or intellectual assets at risk.

Problem Resolution

This provision is about how the organization and outsourcing firm will resolve any disputes and problems. It requires the outsourcing firm to agree to follow the organization's dispute resolution process. This may also include what the procedures would be if the organization and outsourcing firm could not resolve their problems, such as mediation or arbitration. When a problem gets to arbitration, the relationship has usually disintegrated to a point where it cannot be restored.[1]

Quality and Service Level

This provision is about the standards that will be used to judge the quality of materials, courses, or curriculum developed by the outsourcing firm. The language in the master agreement usually characterizes this as the warranty the outsourcing firm will meet for goods and services delivered. It is customary to warrant that the goods and services will meet the standards of the industry, those published by a professional association, or regulated by a government body. The organization may have its own standards. For example, the outsourcing firm must agree to deliver goods specified by the contract that perform as expected, are compatible, contain the specified content, and satisfy any relevant standards, such as instructional design, or conform to SCORM. If the master agreement is silent on standards, the organization has no basis for criticizing the outsourcing firm's work.

This provision also references the standards used to judge service level and it might specify what the qualifications have to be of the people working on the project, how many qualified people are assigned to the services to be provided, the timing of their availability, and the frequency of their availability.

Timeliness and Termination

This provision requires the outsourcing firm to deliver services or goods within the time specified by the master agreement and includes the time limit of the project, whether or not it can be extended or renewed, and for how long or how many times.

DRAFT ADDENDA   Addenda might be created at the same time as the master agreement or may be added later when additional products or services are needed. There should be an addendum for each major deliverable. All addenda are covered by the terms and conditions of the master agreement. The addendum is more detailed and covers specific services or deliverables. For example, if the request for services in the master agreement reads:

> Performance Management Support and Facilitation—expertise in providing assistance to the company's managers and work groups to maintain or improve their performance in a constantly changing environment. This includes identifying and improving critical business and work processes . . .

the addendum might read:

The company is seeking assistance in developing training on a newly engineered work order process used by the maintenance and engineering departments. The training must include (1) learning objectives; (2) a content outline that the procedures for operating the new maintenance and repair system, how the system interfaces with the materials inventory system, and its role in accurately tracking and recording time and materials; (3) learner materials, including practice exercises on the system; and (4) an instructor outline.

The company might create a second addendum for the concession management process, and it might read:

The company is interested in documenting its concession management process to establish standard operating procedures across both facilities and develop performance support tools for contract administration.

The outsourcing firm that was awarded the outsourcing contract to provide performance management support and facilitation would prepare two statements of work describing how it would satisfy each request and at what cost, as shown in Figure 5.4.

AGREE ON TERMS AND CONDITIONS

Some contractual provisions are especially important when outsourcing training, specifically:

1. Accountability
2. Budget
3. Fees
4. Flexibility
5. Quality Statement
6. Service Level Statement

Accountability

This is a description of the roles and responsibilities of the outsourcing firm's personnel, its subcontractors, and the internal training staff. The description should clarify who has the authority to make what type of decisions. For example, it should clarify who has the authority to set work schedules and prioritize tasks, approve content and layout, sign off on usability tests, and spend money. If the organization outsourced the training function as a whole, this provision might specify:

Figure 5.4. Hierarchy
of Contract Elements
with Examples

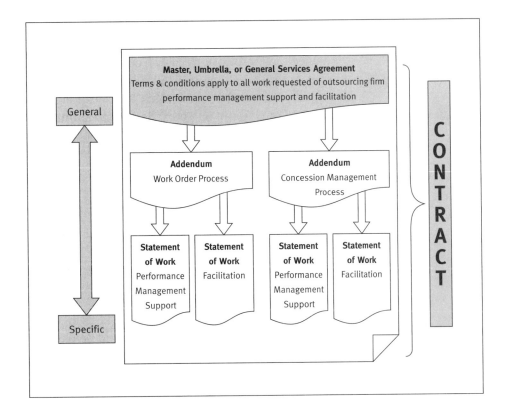

Figure 5.4. Hierarchy of Contract Elements with Examples

1. Who at the organization is authorized to speak on behalf of the company and sign official documents. Who at the organization is to be notified of changes, schedules, project plans, and the like, and who is to receive the deliverables.

2. The job duties of the highest-ranking person on the outsourcing firm's staff assigned to this contract, sometimes referred to as the vendor's "contracting officer."

3. Job duties and reporting relationships of the remaining members of the outsourcing firm's staff and its subcontractors.

4. Any limits on how much money the outsourcing firm can commit before submitting a budget request to the organization's procurement department.

Whether the whole training function is outsourced or not, a provision might be added that requires that a business case or justification be developed and approved before resources, either people and money, are committed.

Budget

When the training function is outsourced, the budget at the master agreement level might be expressed in terms of a total dollar figure, such as $77 million.

The master agreement might contain a provision requiring the outsourcing firm to develop an annual operating and capital budget that is submitted to finance for approval and that the outsourcing firm may not go over budget without approval. If the outsourcing firm is contracted to develop a discrete number of web-based modules, the master agreement might contain a provision requiring the outsourcing firm to submit a budget for the project as a whole. An addendum might be added that requires the budget to be linked to specific deliverables. At some level, the budget, whether it is for managing the whole function or for developing specific courses, should distinguish fixed and variable costs.

Fees

The contract should specify the fees, as well as what fees are and are not included. For example, some organizations will not pay for travel time, but they will pay for travel costs if the travel is on their behalf. The contract also includes any restrictions, for example, that only coach fares will be reimbursed.

Payment terms describe on what basis and for what services the outsourcing firm can bill. Payment terms should be based on deliverables or work performed, not on time.

The contract should specify *penalties,* for example, if all or some percentage of a payment will be withheld for non-performance and if all or just specific requirements are not satisfied.

Flexibility

An outsourcing contract is a long-term commitment, ranging from three to five years. It is difficult to accurately determine the amount or type of work that might have to be done over that period of time. Circumstances may necessitate the need for more or fewer deliverables and different delivery options. Technology may change so much that new options become available and old options, by comparison, are less economical. The organization or a major division might be purchased by or merge with another enterprise, eliminating the need for specific services. It is important that the contract be written to the level of detail that it does not lock the organization or the outsourcing firm into an unviable position. There should be a provision for how the organization and vendor can make changes to the master agreement.

Quality Statement

The quality statement is another key provision in a contract. In the example of the HR consulting firm that outsourced the creation of two hundred modules for customer support personnel to support the new enterprise-wide system, the quality statement in the master agreement might read:

The outsourcing firm is required to comply with the industry standards as published by the International Board of Standards and ASTD in its creation of all course materials.

The quality statement in the addendum might read:

The outsourcing firm will conduct a task analysis for each module using the DIF (difficulty, importance, and frequency) model. The outsourcing firm will submit a design document for approval to the project lead. The design document will contain (1) the results of the DIF analysis; (2) the learning objectives with the conditions, performances, and criteria; (3) a content outline; (4) a description of the instructional strategy; and (5) the end of course test.

The addendum could further stipulate that each module be developed using software in the public domain, Lectora for example, and be SCORM conformant.

Service Level Statement

The service level statement is one of the more important provisions in an outsourcing contract, as it includes the criteria that will be used to judge the adequacy of the service. The service level statement may appear in the master agreement or in an addendum, depending on whether it applies to all of the work being performed by the outsourcing firm or the work required for a specific set of deliverables. There should be clauses in the master agreement or addendum that specify:

- *Hours of operation*—the hours the outsourcing firm's personnel are available for conference calls, online collaboration, consultation, and technical support or developing courseware. Specifying the hours is especially important when the organization and outsourcing firm are in different time zones or in multiple locations.
- *Staffing levels*—the number of people who will be assigned to the different tasks required over the course of the master agreement or addendum. It is especially important when a team is made up of both external and internal resources, including subcontractors.
- *Capability*—the expected level of proficiency of the people assigned to each position, role, or task. It is not enough to state that the outsourcing firm will make programmers, instructional designers, or graphic artists available. The people have to be competent.
- *Roles*—the different roles the outsourcing firm's people will play. The outsourcing firm will probably provide different specialists, some of whom may continue over the course of the master agreement or addendum, such

as a project manager, and others will only be available when their expertise is required, such as graphic artists, programmers, or facilitators.

THE HR CONSULTING COMPANY

The company wrote its contract in a way that should it (1) not be satisfied with the quality of the work; (2) find that it needed more/fewer modules; or (3) identify a more effective way to deliver or develop the training, it could add an addendum instead of nullifying the whole contract.

A LARGE ORGANIZATION

The organization awarded a long-term multimillion-dollar master agreement for interactive multimedia development. After five years it found the vendor could no longer afford to deliver work at the specified prices and the organization could no longer meet its requirements for teaching cases, reviewing content to assure its accuracy, and compliance with evolving specifications.

The technical capability of the equipment on which the training was based had evolved and become significantly more sophisticated. The organization's policies evolved, and learning design and development standards had changed. The organization and vendor had failed to put in a provision allowing them to renegotiate prices and roles and responsibilities.

TOOL 5.1: GUIDELINES FOR CONTRACTING

Here are some guidelines for helping you partner with your legal, finance, and procurement departments. They are the ones who will create the master agreement and addenda. However, they need information from you to create viable, fair contracts. Continue to work with the selection panel or the steering committee established to provide oversight to the outsourcing process. As a group:

1. Describe what you are outsourcing, that is, management of the whole function, curriculum development for a particular learning audience, facilitation of all instructor-led courses, course development for a particular curriculum, and so forth.

2. Identify the deliverables. If you outsourced the whole function, the deliverables might be budgets, training plans, a talent management program, delivery of current programs, and so forth. Suggest an addendum for each one. What provisions should be developed for the addendum?

3. Read over the list of provisions and identify those you think belong in the master agreement. Your legal department will have the final say; however, you should try to understand the intent behind each one.

Use a table like the one in Figure 5.5 for each major deliverable. Assume you are going to write an addendum for each one. What are the factors you want the addendum to include?

Figure 5.5. Deliverable and Contract Provisions

Main Deliverable		
Provision	**Master Agreement**	**Addendum**
Accountability		
Budget		
Confidentiality		
Copyright Releases (reprint permissions)		
Efficacy		
Exit		
Fees		
Financial Stability		
Flexibility		
Governance		
Indemnification		
Liability Limits		
Ownership of Elements or Learning Objects		
Ownership of Data Gained and Data Bases		
Ownership of Discoveries		
Ownership of Courseware		
Payment Terms		
Penalties		
Problem Resolution		

Figure 5.5. Deliverable and Contract Provisions (Continued)

Provision	Master Agreement	Addendum
Quality Standard		
Reports		
Safety		
Service Level		
Termination		
Timeliness		
Other		

4. Identify the standards you will use to evaluate the quality of the work. Be sure to include industry standards like SCORM and professional standards like those developed for instructional designers and instructors.

5. Meet with representatives of the outsourcing firm to identify the information they require to fully understand the intent of the contract and its provisions. If they have an outsourcing relationship with other organizations, they may be able to suggest language that is helpful to both sides.

6. When you have a good idea of what you need in the contract, work with your legal or contract administration department to write the contract.

Outsourcing Training and Development. Copyright © 2006 by John Wiley & Sons, Inc. Reproduced by permission of Pfeiffer, an Imprint of Wiley. www.pfeiffer.com

IMPLICATIONS

If training functions knew their fully loaded costs and better understood their clients' learning needs, they would be in a much stronger position to justify their existence. Outsourcing enables them to be managed as a business, something most training functions are unable to do under their current circumstances. Perhaps more training functions should set themselves up to be internally sourced, that is, contract with the line organization for specific goods and services. They would have to develop a budget, tighten their processes, specify their deliverables, market their services, and deliver services the line organization valued. Once the training function becomes a major line item in the budget with specified deliverables, it will more likely get the attention of senior management.

MISSTEPS AND OVERSIGHTS

Here are some of the more common oversights that organizations make. They fail to create legally binding contracts that adequately define and document work expectation and requirements. They create so many addenda they risk putting in contradictory terms. They also create the need for a document control system. When contracting with a firm located in a different country, they fail to use the services of lawyers from that country. They think offshore outsourcing firms are legally bound by the laws of the organization rather than their own laws. They develop adversarial contracts, rather than ones that benefit both parties. They do not ask outsourcing firms for suggestions about how to structure the relationship and measure success. Organizations write contracts for today, failing to include provisions to accommodate changes it or the outsourcing firm might experience.

SUMMARY

The contract is analogous to a pre-nuptial agreement. It is written for the future and therefore anticipates changes and disagreements. Contacts are communication vehicles, as they provide an opportunity to define terms and relationships that can so easily be assumed or taken for granted.

WHERE TO LEARN MORE

Block, P. (2000). *Flawless consulting: A guide to getting your expertise used* (2nd ed.). San Francisco, CA: Pfeiffer. This landmark bestseller contains three chapters on contracting. Block addresses both the contracting process and key content of a contract. He takes the consultant's perspective.

Ostberg, K. (1990). *Using a lawyer.* New York: Random House. Check out the chapter on Working with a Lawyer.

NOTE

1. A contract can specify the rules of arbitration the organization and outsourcing firm will follow, for example:

   American Arbitration Association—this group may be perceived as too pro-American if the outsourcing firm is not from the United States.

   International Chamber of Commerce (ICC)—this group is generally thought to be the most neutral; however, it is also thought to be expensive.

   Swiss Rules of International Arbitration administered by the Chamber of Commerce in Zurich.

   United Nations Committee on International Trade Law Arbitration Rules (UNCITRAL). The rules can be administered by other organizations, such as the London Court of International Arbitration.

Phase 1: Identifying the Need	Phase 2: Assessing Capacity and Capability	Phase 3: Selecting the Outsourcing Firm	Phase 4: Contracting	Phase 5: Starting Up	Phase 6: Managing the Relationship	Phase 7: Closing Out
Determine client's needs	Assess strengths	Set the baseline	Prepare the contract	Build contract profile	Provide oversight	Notify about termination
a. shorten cycle times	a. credibility and trust	Define roles and responsibilities	Draft master agreement	Set up governance process	Implement the plan and protocols	Transfer intellectual property
b. deliver more training	b. capacity	Define the requirements	Determine scope of work	Develop management plan and schedule	Share expectations and agree on goals	Return physical property
• regulation	c. capability	Define the selection criteria	a. deliverables	Create communication protocols	Communicate	Reconcile financial obligations
• turnover	d. knowledge and skills	Recruit potential outsourcing firms	b. reporting requirements	Develop document standards and controls	Stay current with needs	Terminate clearances, codes
c. provide greater access to training	e. resources	Issue the RFQ	c. problem resolution	Agree on deliverable standards	Measure and report results	Execute final performance review
d. test learners' knowledge	f. work processes	Issue the RFP	d. quality and service level	Identify intellectual property	Celebrate success	Orient the training function
e. report on workforce capability	g. standards	Convene the panel and decide	e. timeliness and termination	Create transition plan	Improve processes	
f. expanding learning audience	Assess weaknesses		Draft addenda	Create dispute resolution process		
g. honor past and future commitments	Conduct job task analysis		Agree on terms and conditions			
Determine criticality and priority	a. by role		a. Accountability			
	b. by task and skill		b. Budget			
			c. Fees			
			d. Flexibility			
			e. Quality statement			
			f. Service level statement			

Figure 6.1. The Engagement Process, Phase 5: Starting Up

Chapter 6

Starting Up

*T*he focus of this chapter is on Phase 5 of The Engagement Process, shown in Figure 6.1. This is the phase during which the training function and outsourcing firm put plans and protocols in place to manage their relationship. Ideally this phase starts with a face-to-face meeting where both parties begin the process of hammering out the details of how they will work together. The first meeting provides a point in time when both sides start performing in their new roles and begin to build the trust necessary for when they later face contentious issues. This phase lays the foundation for an effective partnership. If specific training processes, rather than the whole training function, are outsourced, the same process is followed; however, portions will just be narrower in scope. The outputs of this phase consist of

1. Build contract profile
2. Set up governance process
3. Develop management plan and schedule
4. Create communication protocols
5. Develop document standards and controls
6. Agree on deliverable standards
7. Identify intellectual property
8. Create transition
9. Create dispute process

Figure 6.2 is an overview of the start-up process. It is an example of who should be involved and what role they play in assuring the relationship gets off on the right track.

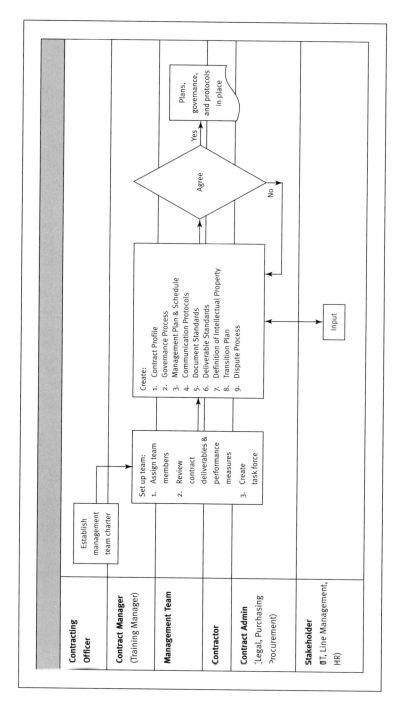

Figure 6.2. The Contract Start-Up Process

BUILD CONTRACT PROFILE

Once the team is in place, each side should create a profile on the other. The profile may contain the highlights of the contract as well. For the outsourcing firm, this entails getting specific contact information on the training function's contract manager. The training function should in turn create a complete profile on the outsourcing firm, similar to what is shown in Tool 6.1.

TOOL 6.1: CONTRACT PROFILE

Information	Description
Name of Outsourcing Firm	The legal name of the outsourcing firm
Contract Number	The number assigned by Procurement
Contract Period	The beginning and ending date (mm/dd/yyyy) of the contract and how many times it may be extended or renewed
Purpose/Description	A description of the goods or services the outsourcing firm is expected to deliver
Outsourcing Firm's Contracting Officer	The name, address, phone number, and email address of the person employed by the outsourcing firm who is authorized to enter into this agreement, sign official documents, etc.
General or Project Manager	The name, address, phone number, and email address of the person who will be onsite to oversee work, whether it is done at the outsourcing firm's site or the training function's site
Emergency Contacts	The names, addresses, phone numbers, and email addresses of other people who are authorized to respond in the case of an emergency
Others	The name, address, phone number, and email address of other people who oversee operations
Hours and Staffing	The days and hours of operation by location. This information is especially important if the contract is to host online access to courses or manage the LMS. Include the expected level of staffing for every service.

Information	Description
Equipment, Utilities, Space	The resources (office space, computers, and peripherals) the organization agrees to provide the outsourcing firm
Performance Bond	The amount of the bond (aggregate sum), the bond number, and the name, address, and phone number of the insurance company, if required
Insurance	The insurance required of the outsourcing firm:
	• Workers' compensation and employer's liability—the state affected, required endorsements, and the dollar amount
	• Commercial liability—dollar amount per occurrence
	• Blanket crime policy—dollar amount per occurrence
	• Auto—carrier, dollar amount
	• Errors and omissions—carrier, dollar amount
	• General liability—carrier, dollar amount
Financial Terms	The fees or expenses to be paid under the contract
	How often invoices can be submitted
	How many copies
	What supporting documents are required—receipts, time sheets (originals or copies)
Changes	How or on what basis the training function or outsourcing firm can modify, formally change, or amend the contract, for example, changes to:
	• Number of deliverables
	• Types of deliverables
	• Minimum and maximum limits on the level of staffing
	• Hours of operation
	• Fees or rates

SET UP GOVERNANCE PROCESS

The governance process is about how decisions are made, priorities are determined, and problems are resolved. Figure 6.3 illustrates a typical governance structure.

Figure 6.3. Typical Governance Structure

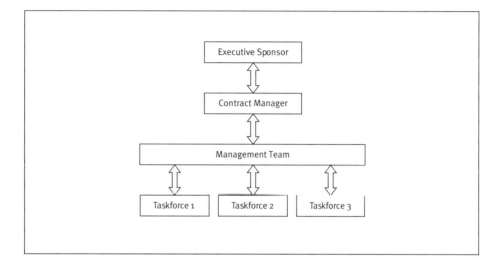

Executive Sponsor

The executive sponsor may be the organization's contracting officer or someone from senior management who is responsible for the outsourcing arrangement and has the ultimate decision-making authority. The role of the executive sponsor is

- To legitimize the relationship with the outsourcing firm
- To provide a charter clarifying the role, scope of authority, and boundaries of the contract manager and management team
- To review the work of the management team and provide counsel if necessary
- To approve any resource allocations on the organization's side
- To be a spokesperson for the relationship
- To mediate disputes

Contract Manager

The contract manager is usually appointed or agreed to by the executive sponsor and is responsible for the day-to-day oversight and coordination of the outsourcing effort. Depending on the scope of the contract, the contract manager may be a full-time assignment. When the entire training function is outsourced, the contract manager (CM) may be someone on the outsourcing firm's staff; otherwise he or she is usually the director of training, chief learning officer, or the director of HR. If only part of the training function's work is outsourced, it might be the head of the training function, someone from IT, or a major stakeholder. The contract manager's role is analogous to a program manager. The responsibilities include:

- Chairing meetings of the management team
- Serving as a liaison between the management team, the executive sponsor, and any task forces
- Coordinating the activities of all task forces or teams
- Maintaining the project/program calendar
- Communicating formally and informally with key stakeholders
- Giving periodic reports to senior management and other stakeholders

Management Team

The management team is made up of an equal number of representatives from the organization and the outsourcing firm. The job of the management team is to assure overall coordination of the individuals and task forces/teams engaged in creating the deliverables. The management team is responsible for:

- Understanding their level of authority and what decisions to escalate to the sponsor
- Assuring there is a communications plan and vehicles (websites, newsletters, and so forth) to announce the new relationship and report ongoing progress
- Developing protocols to help the management team and task forces coordinate and collaborate with each other
- Defining the quality standards that will be used to judge the adequacy of work
- Creating a management plan and schedule
- Designing and overseeing the transition plan or process
- Reviewing progress and ensuring that goals and quality standards are met
- Providing a platform to discuss and resolve issues
- Reviewing requests to change the terms or conditions of the contract and add addenda

The outsourcing firm should identify the people it wants on the management team. At a minimum it should designate someone as its contracting officer with the authority to sign agreements and a contract manager who can commit and schedule staff and recruit specialists as needed.

Depending on the size and scope of the contract, the contract manager may ask others to participate on the management team when it is discussing specific issues or making key decisions. The management team might create task forces to work on specific deliverables. Who participates on the task forces depends on the number and type of specialists required to do the work.

Task Forces

Task forces may be created for each addendum or deliverable, depending on the complexity and scope of the work. When the whole function is outsourced, the task forces are made up of specialists assigned by the outsourcing firm and who may be employees or subcontractors.

THE RETAILER

The retailer set up contracts with two firms. One firm was awarded a multi-year contract to develop a web-based curriculum for the stores. The curriculum would include training of cashiers, head of food service, store managers, and pharmacy technicians. A second one-year contract was awarded to a firm to develop computer-based training for cosmeticians.

The manager of L&D systems training was the contract manager for both contracts. Serving on the management team were the manager of operations training, manager of leadership development, a manager from IT (since the training had to run on the retailer's systems), and one of the lead designers of the store curriculum. Both outsourcing firms appointed a contract officer and a lead designer to the management team.

THE MANUFACTURER OF HEAVY EQUIPMENT

The manufacturer outsourced the development of its complete web-based service-training curriculum to one firm and the development of a worldwide certification program for technicians to an individual consultant. It entered into a contract with the outsourcing firm developing the service training. A letter of agreement was developed for the consultant.

The manager of service training was made contract manager and had oversight of the development of the service-training curriculum. He asked the manager of certification, manager of curriculum development, and manager of material production to serve on the management team. The outsourcing firm appointed a contract officer and two lead designers, one with instructional design expertise and one with web-based training expertise, to serve on the management team.

For the certification project, the manufacturer set up a steering committee to oversee the creation of the certification that was chaired by the manager of certification. Also on the committee were the head of service training, the head of field service, manager of curriculum and material production, a specialist in processes, and the consultant.

THE MIDWEST COMPANY

The company outsourced all design, development, and production of its training curriculum to one outsourcing firm. The director of L&D retained the position of sponsor. The outsourcing firm assigned someone to be the contract manager to chair the management team. To represent the company, the managers responsible for each addendum were on the team. The outsourcing firm had an equal number of project managers. A production manager who worked for the outsourcing firm was responsible for the work of the designers and developers, who were located more than 1,000 miles away from the company's headquarters.

HR CONSULTING COMPANY

The company outsourced the development of its web-based product training for its customer service centers to a firm located in another country.

The manager of systems training was made contract manager, and she also served as the relationship manager. On her committee were the training manager for the customer support call centers, a representative from IT, and a manager of one of the call centers. The outsourcing firm sent fifty specialists to the firm's offices to work directly with IT and subject-matter experts. The specialists reported to a lead designer, who served as the outsourcing firm's contract manager. The lead designer also coordinated the efforts of the project manager, who oversaw the programming that was done in another country.

DEVELOP MANAGEMENT PLAN AND SCHEDULE

One of the responsibilities of the management team is to create a management plan that describes how the outsourcing firm and training function will work together and how the contract manager will provide oversight of the contract. Tool 6.2 has the more common elements that go into a management plan.

TOOL 6.2: MANAGEMENT PLAN GUIDELINES

1. A schedule for when, where, and how often the management team will meet in person or electronically.

2. A list or description of the outsourcing firm's deliverables.

3. A timetable or schedule of how frequently the outsourcing firm is expected to produce the deliverables, including reports. Here is a sample of possible deliverables and reports:

   a. Design documents

   b. Content outlines

   c. Curriculum plans

   d. Prototype layouts

   e. User and usability test methods and results

   f. Storyboards

   g. Progress toward milestones

   h. Course registration and completion reports

   i. Budget report

   j. Course evaluation reports

4. A master calendar showing milestones, deliverables' due dates, and holidays throughout the world.

5. The service level agreement and the quality standards that will be used to judge compliance with the deliverables.

6. How the contract manager will exercise due diligence or quality assurance, that is, validate the work of the outsourcing firm and assure the intent of the work is effective. The activities might include:

   • Direct observation—actually sit in on meetings, interview subject-matter experts, run usability tests, and so forth.

   • Independent tests of the courseware or technology—run parallel yet independent tests to see whether the products or services perform as expected, perhaps with the IT department.

   • Poll clients—interview clients about the outsourcing firm's behavior. This might include asking if the outsourcing firm came prepared for meetings, followed an agenda, followed up on commitments, and used subject-matter experts' time wisely.

THE MANUFACTURER OF HEAVY EQUIPMENT

The management team decided to meet weekly, alternating between the manufacturer's site and the outsourcing firm's site. The team developed a three-year project plan indicating key milestones by curriculum. The process of building the plan helped the team set priorities as to which curriculum to complete first, second, and so forth. They agreed to build the core curriculum on hydraulics and electronics first, as the topics crossed all product lines. Next, they decided which product line to focus on. The process of planning the project allowed the manufacturer to create a new addendum to the contract for each curriculum and incorporate modifications based on what was learned and accomplished on the previous work.

The team used the project plan to schedule specialists to be onsite to do the task analysis and strategize how to inform dealerships around the world of the availability of the curriculum.

THE AIRPORT

The airport's management team put together a three-year plan. The team decided to identify at least two core processes to be reengineered a year. It decided to issue a work order for each process once it was identified. It also anticipated the elimination of specific jobs about nine months into the contract and decided to issue a work order for outplacement services at that time. Different types of specialists were identified during the process of writing the contract for organizational and professional development services.

THE HR CONSULTING FIRM

The firm outsourced the development and production of two hundred modules on how to use the new enterprise-wide system at the call centers to an outsourcing firm in another country. The process of creating a management plan helped the team identify points at which the outsourcing firm's work depended on the completion of work by IT. The team used that information to decide in what order to develop the modules, when and how to best share the information with the developers, and which call centers to use as pilots when implementing the new curriculum. The management plan became a very important control document. As a result, the outsourcing firm was in a better position to schedule its specialists, who were also supporting other customers.

CREATE COMMUNICATION PROTOCOLS

In addition to a management plan and schedule, the management team should develop protocols on how they and the people doing the work will communicate with each other. The protocols should also provide guidance on how designers and specialists will communicate with subject-matter experts, representatives of the learning audience, and other stakeholders. When two organizations begin work together, they face the dilemma of how to best communicate with each other to assure efficient coordination and avoid misunderstandings. The challenge becomes even more difficult when the people involved are in multiple locations across different time zones. A solution is to develop a set of communication protocols.

Protocols are rules of behavior or conduct. They can be thought of as diplomatic guidelines. There are five types of rules:

1. *When and how to communicate within and across teams.* These guidelines address decisions such as when to do conference calls, send emails, forward voice mail, meet in person, post information on a website, and so forth. They include suggestions about the best times to schedule meetings (in person, on the phone, or a live web-cast). They also include suggestions about who to include in conference calls and meetings. People should be included if they have something to contribute or there will be an opportunity for them to add insight or recommendations. However, if the intent is just to inform them, do a data dump; then maybe they can be sent an email or the conversation can be taped for them to listen to at a more convenient time, or put the information on a website to be read or downloaded when convenient. The rules also cover suggestions as to when to call someone at home, on weekends, and on holidays.

2. *Guidelines for collaborating.* These are the rules for how and in what sequence to forward work to the next person in the development, production, or the approval sequence. For example, the person drafting the text of learning materials can forward the work to the person doing animation, who can then forward the work to the person integrating text and graphics. Virtual teams not only require systems or websites that facilitate collaboration, but they need a way to post their work so other team members can contribute their expertise. They are also helped by protocols on when and how to interface electronically with each other.

3. *Guidelines for keeping people informed.* These are the rules about when to copy something for someone. The protocol might specify when and how to indicate if an action or a decision is required. There are a number of benefits to developing communication protocols. For example, they can

reduce the inclination to copy everyone on an email or forward voice mail to everyone. They reduce the incidents of some people having to participate in conference calls at 2 a.m. or on weekends and holidays when all they have to do is listen.

4. *Guidelines for interfacing with the line organization.* Communication protocols can also be used to legitimize the outsourcing firm's people contacting line managers or workers who are subject-matter experts. A protocol might specify that before asking to interview or observe someone, the outsourcing firm should send an email to the person's boss or copy the contract manager or design lead. The protocol might specify what information to put in the email, for example, how the outsourcing firm's representative should introduce him- or herself, explain the purpose of the contact, ask permission to talk to the subject-matter expert, ask for convenient times, provide an estimate on how long the interview or observation will be, and so forth.

5. *Guidelines related to access to proprietary information.* There may be occasions when a course developer or designer will need access to the organization's proprietary information, such as customer data, employee data, formulas, processes, and the like. Protocols should be set up detailing who is authorized to release the data, who is authorized to see or have access to the data, if and how the data might be removed or used by the outsourcing firm and for how long, and what the procedures are for returning or destroying copies of the data. The contract manager has an obligation to assure due diligence is exercised in situations in which access to proprietary data might put the organization at risk.

Tool 6.3 contains a sample of a communications protocol developed by a management team to provide better guidance about when and how to communicate between meetings and with other teams.

TOOL 6.3: SAMPLE COMMUNICATION PROTOCOLS

General

1. Consider and respect global holidays.

2. Before communicating information and selecting the best medium, consider:

   Urgency of message

   Length of message

Accessibility of message to the recipient

Accessibility of tools available to sender

3. Avoid calling a person's cell phone when his or her work phone is busy.

Voice Mail

1. When using voice mail, organize your thoughts ahead of time and keep the message brief and to the point; adhere to the two-minute limit. Do not send long messages in multiple voice mails.

2. Preface voice mail with its purpose (for example, "for your action" or "for your information").

3. Always put long voice mail distribution lists at the end of a message.

4. Limit voice mails during vacation/holiday/weekend periods to business-critical issues, as voice mails will not be reviewed until employees return to work.

5. Refrain from sending meeting minutes via voice mail.

Email

1. Preface email subject with purpose [that is, "for your action" (FYA) or "for your information" (FYI)].

2. Limit emails during vacation/holiday/weekend periods to business-critical issues, as emails will not be reviewed until employees return to work.

3. Reduce attachments in emails; put short, bulleted actions in the main body.

Meetings and Conference Calls

1. Have an agenda.

2. Start on time and end on time.

3. Be courteous, as others may be waiting to use the conference room.

4. Establish meeting norms.

5. Be on time for meetings.

6. Ensure meetings are value added:

Evaluate mandatory participation requirements.

If meeting attendance is poor, find root cause.

7. The person responsible for setting up the conference call or other technology to be used during the meeting should have the technology up and running at least ten minutes prior to start of meeting.

8. All parties dialing into a conference call should dial in two to five minutes prior to the start of the meeting.

9. During conference calls, ask participants to identify themselves when beginning to speak.

10. Minimize cell phone interruptions during meetings to critical issues only.

11. Listen to what people have to say; don't cut people off in the midst of speaking.

12. Be aware that English may be a second language for many global participants:

    Listen for the message rather than the way it is expressed.

    Speak clearly and slowly.

    Avoid using slang and regional idioms.

    Meeting leader should paraphrase inputs for all participants.

13. Respect time zone differences; plan no critical activities for Fridays and Sundays, or share the inconveniences.

    A Monday morning meeting in Chicago at 10 a.m. Central Time is 1 a.m. Tuesday in Tokyo.

14. Don't require frequent meeting updates just to check on progress.

15. Don't call people on cell phones during their non-business hours unless business-critical.

16. Reduce the number of internal meetings. If there's a weekly staff meeting, reduce it by one per month (leave one week open to get work done).

17. Meeting participants should avoid performing other work during meetings and calls.

Another tool that can help when developing protocols is to create a role chart, or a RASCI chart, similar to the one in Tool 6.4. A RASCI chart lists tasks and activities and shows who is responsible (R), who has authority (A), who can provide support (S), who might provide council (C), and who should be kept informed (I).

TOOL 6.4: ROLE AND RESPONSIBILITY CHART

Task, Activity	Person 1	Person 2	Person 3	Person 4
Task Analysis	RA	CS		I
Content Outline	A	S	I	
Design Document				

R = is responsible for the task or activity

A = has approval authority for the task or activity

S = can provide support in the execution of the task or activity

C = can provide council or input on the task or activity

I = should be informed or kept current on the status or decisions related to the task or activity

THE HR CONSULTING FIRM

The contract manager was receiving complaints from IT and call center managers about being copied on too many emails. One call center manager complained about getting copied on over six hundred emails and forty voice mails. The outsourcing firm's project coordinator complained about his people being asked to participate in conference calls on Friday evenings. One of the people in IT complained about receiving a call at 2 a.m. about one of the programs.

The management team investigated the underlying reasons for the complaints. The team realized that people were unclear about who needed what information and in what format. The result was that course developers were trying to keep everyone else informed, only to cause unnecessary work, delays, and hard feelings. The management team drafted some communication protocols to resolve the problems.

DEVELOP DOCUMENT STANDARDS AND CONTROLS

Document standards are similar to communication protocols in that they define the purpose of the report, who has sign-off authority, the preferred format, the preferred medium, to whom they are sent, and how frequently. Over the course of the engagement, numerous documents will be created and revised, including status reports, budgets, project plans, staffing plans, business cases, and the like. A document control system needs to be set up to assure people work with the most recent and approved versions. Documents, whether they are electronic or paper, can provide an audit trail and facilitate decision making. The management team should identify the types of reports it wants, the format, the level of detail desired, who is authorized to approve them, and a document control system.

AGREE ON DELIVERABLE STANDARDS

The contract usually lists the expected deliverables, such as proof of concept, curriculum design, course design documents, learning objectives, content outlines, test questions, graphics, game rules, storyboards, and so forth. However, the format of these deliverables and the amount and level of detail of the information they contain is usually not specified. The lack of guidance can result in misunderstandings and hard feelings. One way to assure the outsourcing firm meets the expectations of the organization is to mutually agree on standards, templates, or requirements.

Standards and templates provide guidance to course developers, graphic artists, and all the other specialists involved in creating learning materials. Curriculum and course development are processes whereby learning content and instructional tactics are transformed from a conceptual stage to a final production stage. At each stage another specialist adds his or her expertise. Standards facilitate collaboration and prevent rework and misunderstandings. Tool 6.5 is an example of the level of information expected in design documents and learning objectives.

TOOL 6.5: STANDARDS FOR DELIVERABLES

Design Document Standards

Design documents should contain the following information:

1. Description of the learning audience

2. Prerequisites: What is the person expected to know and be able to do before beginning training?

3. Description of the learning plan: required pre-work, self-study, number of modules, lessons, or courses; relationship to or sequence in the curriculum

4. Description of the delivery method(s) and media

5. Description of the instructional strategy

6. The learning objectives

7. The content outline

8. Assessment method

Learning Objectives Standards

Learning objectives should contain the following information:

1. The major content (topic) areas to be covered in the training

2. The conditions

   • What information, tools, materials, equipment, and other resources will the person have access to during the learning event?

   • What will be the training environment and how closely does it conform to the job environment?

3. The performance statement(s).

   • What does the person have to demonstrate for you to accept that learning has occurred?

   • What do you want the person to know or do after completing the training?

4. The criteria

   • What standards will be applied to judge whether or not the person learned what was expected and to the appropriate degree?

THE HEAVY EQUIPMENT MANUFACTURER

The outsourcing firm conducted a comprehensive task analysis of all the service technicians' jobs across all the product lines. The level of detail was immense. The outsourcing firm's course developers took the data from the task analysis and began developing web-based courses. The outsourcing firm believed it had met the terms of the agreement that asked for a task analysis and courses. However, the course developers bypassed the step of creating a curriculum design that included the courses and modules and course objectives.

At the same time as the course developers were building the modules, another team was charged with creating pre- and post-tests for each module. The failure to stipulate the need for a curriculum and course objectives made the job of the test developers more difficult, as they were unable to determine at what level to write the test questions and what module covered what content. The management team realized the need to specify the requirements for each deliverable expected of the outsourcing firm, including the level of detail required and in what format.

IDENTIFY INTELLECTUAL PROPERTY

A subject that causes significant confusion is intellectual property, specifically what it is and who owns it. It is very important that the management team define intellectual property and establish rules related to ownership early in the relationship. There are at least four dimensions to intellectual property, including the following.

Final Deliverables or Courseware

The courseware or final deliverables are the curriculum, courses, and modules created by the outsourcing firm as part of the contract, independent of the delivery medium. This is what the training function buys and learners experience. Ownership of the final deliverables seems on the surface relatively clear cut; however, problems occur when the outsourcing firm creates similar products for other clients or purchases courseware for a one-time or limited use on behalf of the training function.

Learning Objects or Components

Learning objects are all the components that went into the creation of the courseware. Ownership of the learning objects becomes an issue when the training function wants to revise, update, or modify the courseware at a later date. When the outsourcing firm creates the objects on behalf of the training function, ownership becomes clearer. However, outsourcing firms are frequently selected because of their industry experience, which could mean they are reusing objects or buying objects created by others. The firm may have commissioned, bought, or leased the rights to the learning objects. When this is the case, the rights to use, much less modify, the objects becomes less clear. Here are some examples:

- Text and written dialogue that are used in audio and video scripts, narrations, and the learners' reading materials, such as in the explanations, practice exercises, instructions, summaries, and the like

- Visuals, including drawings, renderings, photographs, and schematics that are incorporated into learner materials to illustrate, demonstrate, and provide learners' practice of rules, concepts, and relationships, procedures, and the like

Tools Used in Creation and Revision

The outsourcing firm uses tools to create and assemble the objects into courseware. The tools include the technology and software used to author, program, film, tape, generate graphics, produce animation, and do video and audio recordings and editing. The training function must either own or be able to access the tools and technology to revise, update, or modify the courseware. If the tools and technology are proprietary, the training function can only gain access by paying a licensing fee. This is why more organizations are requiring outsourcing firms to only use technology that is in the public domain and can be purchased.

Data Gained and Databases Created

The outsourcing firm will normally acquire data or intelligence about learners, the content of the courseware, the organization's customers, and the like. The data are acquired during (1) interviews, observations, and surveys used to do needs and job task analyses; (2) the administration of tests and course registrations; and (3) the delivery of classroom and online courses. The training function may believe it owns the data; however, unless the contract stipulates who owns what data, ownership could be in question, especially when the outsourcing firm wants to use the data for other engagements or purposes.

It is essential that the management team set up an inventory or cataloguing system whereby all courseware, learning objects, tools and technology, and data are catalogued, named according to naming conventions, and inventoried. However, it is essentially impossible to identify all of the intellectual property that will be created or acquired during the course of the engagement; therefore, the management team must create procedures or protocols that will be followed whenever it commissions the outsourcing firm to develop courses, conduct analyses, administer any training events, and manage the administration of training records. Tool 6.6 is a set of guidelines for defining intellectual property and clarifying ownership issues.

TOOL 6.6: IDENTIFICATION OF INTELLECTUAL PROPERTY

Dedicate time with the management team to develop a way to identify, define, catalogue, and inventory intellectual property that may be produced during the term of the contract. Include someone from the legal department as appropriate. Understand it will be practically impossible to identify all of the intellectual property that will be created or acquired over the course of the contract; however, the team can put in place methods and procedures to help.

1. Review the provisions in the contract about intellectual property. See whether there is a clause requiring the outsourcing firm to (a) identify the learning objects used in the creation of courseware and their source and/or (b) use tools and technology that are in the public domain. Confirm that any data collected or compiled in the course of developing courseware is owned by the organization.

2. For each addendum, specific course, or project, arrange for the outsourcing team and representatives of the training function to create a database for capturing data, recording learning objects and their source, and recording the tools and technology to be used.

3. During the development of courseware, assign someone the responsibility of recording what learning objects were created or acquired and their source and assuring that all reprint agreements are on file.

4. During any analysis or administration of the training, assign someone the responsibility of identifying any data collected.

5. At the time courseware or the results of an analysis are complete, have someone from the management team confirm that the record of courseware, learning objects, tools used, and data captured is complete and accurate.

6. If the outsourcing firm had created similar courseware for another client, assure the firm has a plan for how it will differentiate your work from that done for other customers. The plan might include file naming conventions or different domains on a server.

CREATE TRANSITION PLAN

Outsourcing is all about shifting or sharing responsibilities; however, the shift does not happen naturally and may take months to accomplish. Therefore, the transition plan should first identify what has to take place for the outsourcing firm to be able to assume the responsibilities expected of it. The management team is in the best position to define what a completed transition entails and set an expected time frame. To do this, it should begin with the end in mind and backward chain, listing the decisions to be made, events to be completed, and any processes, protocols, and technology to be built or acquired. The plan is made more complex if it involves the organization eliminating positions and laying people off and, similarly, the outsourcing firm hiring or contracting project managers and specialists. Whenever hiring, firing, recruiting, or relocating is required, more people have to be involved, such as HR and the legal department. Whenever major acquisitions are required, such as a LMS or an enterprise-wide database system, finance, procurement, and end users have to be involved. The plan should indicate when other groups are involved and the decisions or actions that have to be made for the transition to be successful.

Transition plans are more likely to succeed, that is, happen with fewer mishaps, if they are very detailed. For example, if the outsourcing firm's people will work at the organization's location, then identification badges and parking passes have to be arranged. This requires scheduling photo sessions, background checks, drug tests, and the like. If people are going to be displaced, then decisions have to be made about outplacement, severance, and training the replacements who might be employees of the outsourcing firm. If the outsourcing firm's people are to work collaboratively with people in the training function, then roles and responsibilities have to be clearly defined, quality standards and templates agreed on. It may be necessary to conduct an orientation for the outsourcing firm's people so they can be quickly brought up-to-speed on the organization, its products, processes, and systems. Tool 6.7 contains questions to be asked when developing a transition plan.

TOOL 6.7: TRANSITION PLAN QUESTIONS

Question	Response
What is the target end date for having the transition complete?	
What learning content must the outsourcing firm become proficient in?	
Who will be responsible for bringing them up-to-speed?	
What equipment and systems must the outsourcing team gain an understanding of?	

Question	Response
Who will be responsible for training them?	
What decisions must be made?	
• Roles and responsibilities	
• Purchases	
• Personnel	
• Systems	
Who makes these decisions?	
What processes, protocols, or standards have to be created for the outsourcing firm to do its work?	
Who will do it?	
What purchases have to be made before the outsourcing firm can begin its work?	
When will they be made?	
What must be done for the outsourcing firm to gain access to the content, subject-matter experts, systems, and so on?	
• Pass codes	
• Badges	
• Drug tests	
What personnel actions have to be carried out for the transition to be complete?	
• Outplacement	
• Severance	
• Relocation	
• Recruiting	
• Orientation	
Who is responsible for doing them?	
What must be in place for completion?	

THE MIDWEST COMPANY

The company had outsourced the design, development, and production of its technical curriculum to a vendor located 1,000 miles away. For the outsourcing firm to be successful, the company had to plan on how to transfer or make accessible the learning content, which included all of the company's products. The product mix was very complex. In the past the instructional designers worked closely with engineering and product support. The decision was made to set up virtual teams that included curriculum managers who worked for the company and designer developers who worked for the outsourcing firm. The virtual teams were assigned one or more product lines. The management team, in conjunction with the virtual teams, met to plan out how they would work together. It took them almost three months to work out the details of the relationship, including:

- Defining or designing standards and templates
- Defining the product deliverables
- Deciding on the reporting requirements
- Developing interface protocols
- Clarifying roles and responsibilities
- Developing project plans
- Becoming oriented with the company's intranet and IT requirements

In parallel with these decisions, the designers and developers who were laid off were offered employment opportunities with the outsourcing firm, but the offer did not include a relocation allowance. Those who did not move were offered outplacement services.

CREATE DISPUTE RESOLUTION PROCESS

It is the management team's role to resolve problems; when this does not happen, the sponsor can render an opinion. However, when the sponsor is reluctant or the management team is deadlocked, another process needs to be available. The dispute resolution process is an alternative course of action that should be in place before the need arises. The contract should include an agreement, in principle, to resolve disputes. However, the management team will still need to develop details for the dispute resolution process.

The dispute resolution process can allow for one or more levels of appeal. For example, one approach is to agree to set up a panel to hear the dispute and abide by the panel's decision. Another approach is to start with a panel, but allow the parties to agree to mediation or arbitration if they cannot accept the panel's decision or recommendation. Figure 6.4 is an example of a dispute resolution process. Tool 6.8 contains some the questions that should be asked when designing a dispute resolution process.

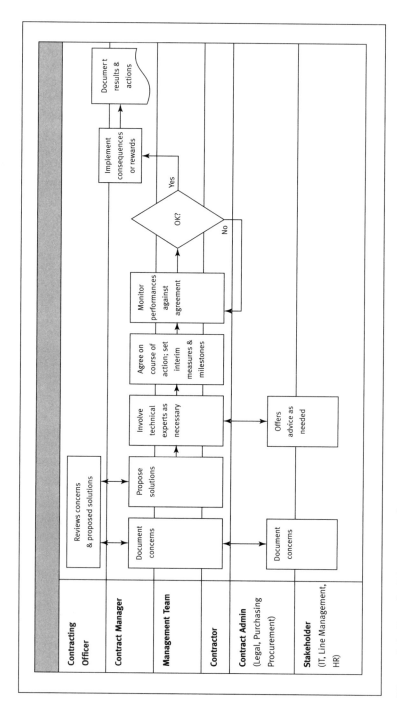

Figure 6.4. Sample Dispute Resolution Process

TOOL 6.8: DISPUTE RESOLUTION QUESTIONS

1. How long after the incident do the parties have before engaging the dispute resolution process?

2. Must the management team or sponsor refer the problem to the dispute resolution process or can the parties bypass them?

3. How many people should hear the dispute, an even number with equal representation from both sides, or an odd number?

4. What attributes or characteristics must people satisfy to be qualified to "hear" the dispute, including the panel, mediators, and arbitrators?

5. Will the parties be allowed legal representation or do they have to personally present their cases?

6. Will the rules of evidence be in force, such as whether or not hearsay is allowed, each side must disclose its evidence prior to the meeting, and the accused is allowed to see or hear the evidence?

7. How much time will the parties have to present their sides?

8. Where will the dispute be heard, at the training function's site or the outsourcing firm's?

9. Who pays any associated expenses associated with hearing the dispute?

10. Is the decision of the dispute resolution panel final, can a party appeal to a higher level, or can one go to mediation or formal arbitration?

Ideally, the relationship never breaks down to the extent that the dispute process is needed. However, when it is necessary, the rules should be developed when the parties are still friendly.

Tool 6.9 contains some start-up guidelines.

TOOL 6.9: START-UP GUIDELINES

Here are some guidelines designed to help you put in place the processes and protocols for building a successful relationship. Set up a cross-functional team whose members include the training function and the outsourcing firm. Together:

1. Create a contract profile. Share it with the other party to confirm it is accurate and complete. See Figure 6.3 and Tool 6.1.

2. Draft each element in the start-up phase.

a. *A governance process.* Identify the sponsor, contract managers, management team members, and the task forces in the short term and long term. Define the roles and responsibilities of the sponsor, contract managers, and management team. See Figure 6.3.

b. *A management plan and schedule.* Brainstorm what to include in the management plan. Put together a high-level project plan and suggest milestones and delivery dates. See Tool 6.2.

c. *Communication protocols.* Use the one in Tool 6.3 as a model. Be sure to include protocols for using voice mail, email, meetings, and collaboration.

d. *Roles and responsibilities.* Explore developing a roles and responsibilities chart similar to the one in Tool 6.4.

e. *Documentation standards.* Identify the types of documents that are required. Decide on the level of detail required for each one. Decide how the documents are to be generated and by whom. Agree on a document control system and make someone responsible for using it.

f. *Deliverable standards.* As you identify the deliverables, specify the level of detail required, agree on a template, and draft procedures for how virtual teams might collaborate and share work in progress. Build on the standards in Tool 6.5.

g. *Identification of intellectual property.* Follow the guidelines in Tool 6.6. Make identifying, recording, and confirming ownership a priority.

h. *The transition process.* Start with the end in mind. Together brainstorm the most important decisions and events that have to take place before the outsourcing firm has the information, guidance, and work protocols required to do the work. Add to the questions in Template 6.7 and in Figure 6.9.

i. *The dispute resolution process.* What will be the rules for bringing, hearing, resolving, and appealing a dispute? How many levels of appeals do you want? Will the appeal involve mediation or arbitration? What will the final level of appeal be like? Use the outline in Figure 6.4 and the questions in Tool 6.8 to get started.

3. Share your work with the sponsor.

IMPLICATIONS

Outsourcing, particularly when it involves contracting with a firm "off shore" requires new ways of operating and communicating. The models training functions and outsourcing firms have to draw on are flawed at best, particularly when the goal is relationship-based, requiring mutual respect and interdependence versus subservience. The classic customer-vendor model does not support risk taking or innovation. The partnership model is closer, yet still incomplete because it does not fully address the potential disparity of risk and reward. Outsourcing training, all or in part, provides whole new opportunities to redefine business relationships, roles and responsibilities, and risks and rewards.

MISSTEPS AND OVERSIGHTS

One of the more common missteps is to discount the importance of building a foundation for the relationship, clarifying roles and responsibilities, and putting procedures in place that facilitate communication and accountability. The start-up phase could be likened to either the engagement or honeymoon. The parties involved pay a lot of attention to the other person; however, they should use it as an opportunity to look at their own assumptions and behaviors. They enter into the relationship with assumptions about how to change the other players, but unwilling to seriously question their own ways of operating. Another misstep is a failure to seriously build protocols or to define behaviors that support civility and collaboration.

SUMMARY

The contract profile, management plan, protocols, and dispute process are designed to address demands the training function and the outsourcing firm will have to address at some time in the future. A successful relationship takes time. Both parties have to be willing to dedicate the time and care to learn about each other and build tools to help them withstand the challenges they will experience. The better each party understands the needs of the other and is fully prepared to honor commitments, the greater the chances of success. However, trust takes time, which is why laying the groundwork is so important. When the organization just wants to turn over the training function to the outsourcing firm and have minimal involvement, it discounts the outsourcing firm's need to leverage the training function's knowledge of the organization, its people, processes, and products. There is rarely enough time for the outsourcing firm to establish the level of trust and deep understanding required to develop training that is relevant and accurate.

WHERE TO LEARN MORE

Here is a little book based on research that is an easy read. It is about building effective relationships.

Cialdini, R. (2001). *Influence: Science and practice* (4th ed.). Boston, MA: Allyn and Bacon.

Phase 1: Identifying the Need	Phase 2: Assessing Capacity and Capability	Phase 3: Selecting the Outsourcing Firm	Phase 4: Contracting	Phase 5: Starting Up	Phase 6: Managing the Relationship	Phase 7: Closing Out

Determine client's needs
a. shorten cycle times
b. deliver more training
  • regulation
  • turnover
c. provide greater access to training
d. test learners' knowledge
e. report on workforce capability
f. expanding learning audience
g. honor past and future commitments
Determine criticality and priority
	Assess strengths
	a. credibility and trust
	b. capacity
	c. capability
	d. knowledge and skills
	e. resources
	f. work processes
	g. standards
	Assess weaknesses
	Conduct job task analysis
	a. by role
	b. by task and skill
		Set the baseline
		Define roles and responsibilities
		Define the requirements
		Define the selection criteria
		Recruit potential outsourcing firms
		Issue the RFQ
		Issue the RFP
		Convene the panel and decide
			Prepare the contract
			Draft master agreement
			Determine scope of work
			a. deliverables
			b. reporting requirements
			c. problem resolution
			d. quality and service level
			e. timeliness and termination
			Draft addenda
			Agree on terms and conditions
			a. Accountability
			b. Budget
			c. Fees
			d. Flexibility
			e. Quality statement
			f. Service level statement
				Build contract profile
				Set up governance process
				Develop management plan and schedule
				Create communication protocols
				Develop document standards and controls
				Agree on deliverable standards
				Identify intellectual property
				Create transition plan
				Create dispute resolution process
					Provide oversight
					Implement the plan and protocols
					Share expectations and agree on goals
					Communicate
					Stay current with needs
					Measure and report results
					Celebrate success
					Improve processes
						Notify about termination
						Transfer intellectual property
						Return physical property
						Reconcile financial obligations
						Terminate clearances, codes
						Execute final performance review
						Orient the training function

Figure 7.1. The Engagement Process, Phase 6: Managing the Relationship

Chapter 7

Managing the Relationship

*T*he focus of this chapter is on the ongoing management of the relationship, as shown in Phase 6 of The Engagement Process (See Figure 7.1). This is the phase during which the contract manager oversees the relationship and implements the management plan. It is also during this phase that the contract manager, management team, and outsourcing firm celebrate success, address change, work through issues, and solve problems.

Using marriage as an analogy, a lot of attention is paid to the courtship, engagement, wedding ceremony, and honeymoon. However, not a lot of attention is paid to sustaining the marriage. The same thing happens in business. The assumption is that once the contract is signed the relationship will take care of itself. Unfortunately, this is not always the case. Needs change, expectations are forgotten, priorities shift, new players come on board, and new pressures surface. During the Starting-Up Phase, roles were established, specifically those of the contract manager and management team. The management team built plans and protocols the training function and outsourcing firm could use to help guide the relationship and keep it on course. Once the transition is over, those plans and protocols stay in play, and someone has to be responsible for keeping them alive.

PROVIDE OVERSIGHT

Oversight is not about micromanaging or trying to catch the outsourcing firm making mistakes or taking advantage of the organization. It is about both sides honoring their commitment to the relationship, anticipating change, and working to help each other succeed.

IMPLEMENT THE PLAN AND PROTOCOLS

Figure 7.2 is a process map that simplistically describes the mutual responsibilities of the training function and outsourcing firm.

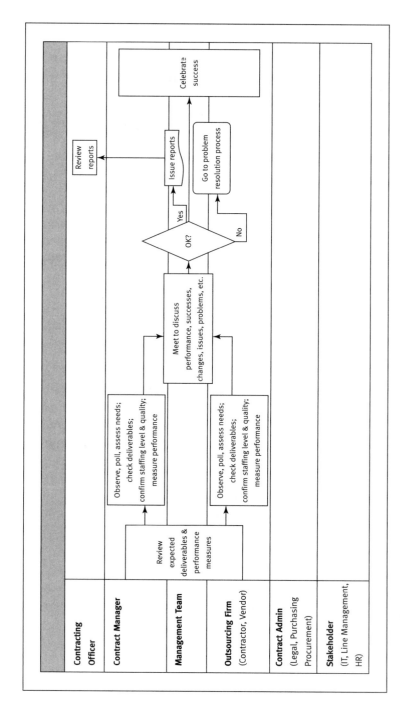

Figure 7.2. The Management Process

The other key actions for a successful relationship include:

- Share expectations and agree on goals
- Communicate
- Stay current with needs
- Measure and report results
- Celebrate success
- Improve processes

SHARE EXPECTATIONS AND AGREE ON GOALS

Maintaining a sense of shared expectations and agreement on the goals may seem easy to do, but it is not. Turnover will occur within the training function, the outsourcing firm, and the team. Incumbents become immersed in the day-to-day demands and can easily be distracted by immediate pressures and lose sight of the priorities. There should be a way to bring new people up-to-speed quickly and periodically revisit the reasons behind outsourcing with incumbents. For example, assume the driver was the need to shorten the time it takes to bring people to proficiency and the plan to do this was to increase the fidelity of the training. However, since the training function lacked the expertise and technology to build robust interactive training, the decision was made to engage an outsourcing firm with the technical capability. Somehow the goal of shortening the time to proficiency needs to stay on the management team's agenda and, assuming the training function established a baseline for how long it took before outsourcing, it should be the ultimate measure for evaluating the effectiveness of the relationship.

Unfortunately, teams assume everyone knows the history behind the relationship and fail to appreciate the need to orient new members and reorient the veterans. The management team and the task forces run the risk of focusing on activities and outputs at the expense of what they were really commissioned to accomplish.

A technique that can be helpful includes creating a standard orientation package that is implemented every time a new task force is created, a new line manager who is responsible for a key learning audience is hired, and/or a new specialist joins the team. The orientation package should be created early in the relationship because the process of building it will surface any misunderstandings and facilitate the group becoming a team.

Tool 7.1 gives some tips on how to create an orientation package and what it might contain.

TOOL 7.1: ORIENTATION GUIDELINES

At some point early in the relationship, meet with the management team and identify the information you think would be useful for new team members, line managers, and task forces as they are commissioned. Some of the things the orientation package might include are listed below. Add items appropriate for your situation.

- The reasons why the organization engaged an outsourcing firm
- A description of the outsourcing firm's capabilities
- The key performance measures or indicators
- An overview of the governance structure
- The rules and responsibilities of the contract manager and management team
- The management team's charter
- The standards that are and will be used to judge work products
- The staffing level agreement
- The immediate and long-term deliverables
- Contact information
- Roles of key players
- Any agreed-on process or protocols
- Other

Outsourcing Training and Development. Copyright © 2006 by John Wiley & Sons, Inc. Reproduced by permission of Pfeiffer, an Imprint of Wiley. www.pfeiffer.com

COMMUNICATE

A standard order given to teams is communicate, communicate, and communicate more. Unfortunately, communicate is interpreted to mean dump data and tell, tell, and tell again. Effective communication is a lot more than telling; it requires the management team and contract manager to engage in dialogue with each other and their team members, that is, the people building training, doing needs assessments, contributing content, and so forth. They should elicit each other's opinions and information and use what they learn to identify any misunderstandings and improve their work. An approach some teams find helpful is to distinguish how they want to communicate with stakeholders and within the team. For example, to better communicate with stakeholders, the team might:

- List the various ways it can keep people up-to-date, such as through a web-site or email or town hall meetings, and then use as many as feasible.

- List the ways stakeholders can express their concerns and pose questions, such as chat rooms, town hall meetings, or inviting representatives to meet with the management team on a periodic basis, and then making a commitment to give their ideas a fair hearing and implement them as appropriate.

- Ask stakeholders how they want to be kept informed and on what issues they want to be involved, and then follow up on their suggestions.

THE MANUFACTURER OF HEAVY EQUIPMENT

The more than two hundred dealerships worldwide set up a Dealership Council. Dealers in each region appoint a representative from their area to sit on the council, which meets quarterly to discuss common issues. The contract manager for the service training suggested appointing a representative from the dealers' council to be on the management team and certification steering committee. He wanted a legitimate way to test out ideas on the dealerships, enlist their help in conducting pilot studies, and hear their expectations about how the training should be structured and the requirements for certification.

In exchange he asked if he could attend council meetings to update the members on service training and technician certification. At his first meeting with the council, the members asked him to develop a process to accredit dealerships that meet a minimum standard for preparing their technicians. As a result, the contract manager set up a taskforce to draft a set of standards and a process for evaluating dealers' training effectiveness.

These approaches address how the team will communicate with people outside the team, but not with each other during or between meetings. Establishing a communication protocol helps, but teams should also set up rules for how they want to conduct their meetings. For example, the contract manager and team might agree to always have an agenda with measurable outcomes or actions, not just a list of topics. The management team's agenda could include time to discuss and debate. The team norms could include listening to divergent opinions and exploring different approaches to meeting the deliverables. The team should make it a point to question its own assumptions.

When someone on the team disagrees with a decision or proposed set of actions, another team member could be appointed to act as an advocate or be responsible for facilitating an exchange of ideas to assure that opposing ideas receive a fair hearing. The advocate's primary role is to prevent the team from becoming polarized, reduced to taking sides, or blaming.

The ideal situation is one in which team members trust one another. Trust has to be earned, and one way that is done is when team members represent each other accurately and fairly. This requires members having the skills to hear the intent behind messages, not just the words that were used. Not everyone is skilled at expressing ideas; sometimes people can come across harshly or as blaming. The key is to believe that the other person only wants the best and is awkward in expressing what he or she wants to happen.

THE AIRPORTS

The management team met every other week for the first year of the contract and changed to meeting once a month thereafter. However, it set up a method whereby the contract manager could call special meetings. She could also poll the members by email if a question or issue arose that could not wait until the regularly scheduled meeting.

The team also decided in advance how it wanted to handle significant disagreements, whether they were about standards, methods, or priorities. Here are some of the provisions it developed to help it avoid personalizing disputes or politicizing disagreements.

They agreed they:

- Would not run to constituents and lobby for support.

- Would work hard to understand all sides of a dispute.

- Would not talk about each other in ways that were disparaging or disrespectful.

- Would agree to disagree and ask the sponsor to mediate or make the final decision.

- Would honor any decision the group or sponsor made.

The team created a flow chart describing the process it would use to resolve problems.

Tool 7.2 has some ways to explore how to communicate with stakeholders and with each other.

TOOL 7.2: COMMUNICATION GUIDELINES

This guideline is in two parts. Part 1 is about communicating with stakeholders. Part 2 is about how the team will communicate with each other during and between meetings.

Part 1: Communicating with Stakeholders

Either during a regularly scheduled management team meeting or a special one, discuss the type of relationship you want with stakeholders and how you want to communicate with them. Use the questions below to assess the current relationship and identify any necessary changes. Add questions and periodically revisit the decisions and commitments you make to assure they are still appropriate.

1. How do we currently communicate with stakeholders?

2. Have we purposely asked them how they want us to communicate with them?

3. Who do we include when we discuss:

   Who our stakeholders are?

   What the desired relationship is?

   How the relationship will be accomplished?

   What the measures of success will be?

4. Do we ask our stakeholders:

   What they expect of the training function?

   What their issues and challenges are?

   What business issues they are facing?

   The learning and performance implications of the business issues?

   How we might stay current on their strategies, markets, products and services, technologies, processes, and goals?

   How to improve our relationship with them?

Part 2: Communicating with Each Other

Prior to a regularly scheduled meeting, ask team members to come prepared to discuss how they want to communicate and engage in dialogue during and between meetings. Use the table below to start the discussion. Add other questions to make the process relevant to your situation. The team may want to describe the process it will follow when discussing issues and resolving problems.

Communicate with Each Other	Comments

1. How do we want to work together as a team?

   Can we agree to respect each other?

   Can we agree to hear each other out and not interrupt?

   Can we agree to maintain confidences?

   Can we agree to represent each other's opinions accurately and respectfully?

2. What might we do to make our meetings efficient?

   Always have an agenda with outcomes and activities?

   Agree to come prepared?

   Ask questions to assure understanding?

   Have the person presenting the problem or recommendation be prepared to address the pros and cons?

3. How will we make decisions?

   By consensus or majority vote?

   By escalating decisions to our sponsor?

4. What is our role in terms of representing constituents?

   Can we agree to act as liaisons with our direct constituents?

   Can we agree to represent our constituents' views, even when we personally disagree?

5. How will we handle issues that come up between meetings?

   Do we want to set up a protocol, such as when to use email, voice mail, or call emergency meetings?

STAY CURRENT WITH NEEDS

One of the greater challenges the management team will face is how to stay current with constituents' needs and new developments in learning technology. The training development cycle time can be extensive and, unfortunately, programs can be quickly outdated. The outsourcing firm's deliverables were probably defined at the time the contact was signed. If the contract calls for the outsourcing firm to conduct periodic needs assessments, there is probably a provision for staying current. This should also be the case when the whole function is outsourced. But if only specific services and deliverables were commissioned, then there is a need to set up a more deliberate way to stay current on the organization's needs and opportunities to leverage new developments in learning technologies.

THE HR CONSULTING FIRM

The management team decided to poll the call centers, marketing, and IT twice a year to identify issues that might require training's support, whether that be a new module or a performance support tool. The method it used was to distribute a short survey on email, and interview in person or by phone the leadership of the three functions. It used the results from the first round to identify any issues in need of further investigation or modification of priorities. It scheduled the second round of surveys and interviews one month before budgets were due. It used the findings from the second round as input when developing its annual operating and capital expense budget.

The management team also developed a master calendar showing all of the major meetings that were scheduled worldwide. It used the calendar to negotiate for a place on the agenda to either update constituents or solicit feedback. The calendar helped the team identify events that someone from the training function or outsourcing team was scheduled to attend or could attend to control travel costs.

TOOL 7.3: GUIDELINES FOR STAYING CURRENT

Put on the agenda the subject of how the management team will stay abreast of stakeholders' needs with an action item to agree on a methodology. Use the questions below to facilitate the discussion. Revisit the group's decisions to assure they are still appropriate. The questions are only a beginning. Adapt them for your own use.

---

1. What will be our strategy or process for staying current about our stakeholders' needs?

2. What will be our approach or process for conducting:

   Needs assessments?

   Job or task analyses?

   Competency studies?

3. Are there any regularly scheduled events we might leverage, such as product meetings?

4. Are there any regularly scheduled events during which we should not compete for people's attention or time, such as the annual sales convention or product showcase meetings for customers?

5. How will we stay abreast of new developments in learning technologies?

6. Whose budget will cover attendance at national or international conferences or expositions?

7. How will budget requests be handled to cover the cost of members of the training function or the outsourcing team attending conferences?

8. How might the training function or the outsourcing firm bring forward recommendations to invest in new technology or products?

MEASURE AND REPORT RESULTS

Another important part of sustaining an effective relationship is deciding in advance how to measure the results of products and services and the relationship itself. At some point in the relationship the measures of success should have been discussed and agreed on. Measuring the outsourcing firm's deliverables starts with listing them and then describing the criteria that will be used to judge quality. Measuring assumes a deliverable will be compared to an agreed-on standard, guideline, template, and so forth. The outsourcing firm deserves knowing what the point of comparison is and may have suggestions to offer.

Evaluation can be done at many levels. For example, the training function and outsourcing firm might decide to focus on measuring the deliverables or products produced during the first year. They might want to set baselines for the processes used in development and production. They could even decide to measure compliance with standards. Evaluation during the second year might include outcomes, such as the average time to bring a new hire to proficiency, reduction in accidents, any change in customer satisfaction ratings, or the average cost to develop one hour of instruction. Whatever the level, the training function and outsourcing firm need to decide:

- What information they want to obtain to support decisions
- What the purpose or goal is of evaluating
- What the measures of success, effectiveness, or efficiency will be
- What the point of comparison or baseline will be
- How they will go about getting the data or information

The management team may want to measure the efficiency of the processes used to create learning products, such as time, cost, and resource consumption. When the goal is compliance, it is helpful to have agreed-on standards, guidelines, and templates. For example, there can be guidelines for processes, such as a documented methodology for doing needs assessments and job task analyses. There can be agreed-on criteria for what design documents and learning objectives must satisfy. Templates can be developed for learning materials, eliminating the need to create new formats for every course. In each of these cases, the training function and outsourcing firm need only determine the frequency with which work products comply with the standards, guidelines, or templates. If the goal is learner acceptance, the training function and outsourcing firm need to track usage and completion rates, end-of-course evaluation results, and the degree to which the learning transferred to the job. Whatever the goal, it is essential that the organization and outsourcing firm decide in advance what the key performance measures or indicators of success will be.

THE HR CONSULTING FIRM

The company outsourced the development of about two hundred modules to a firm in another country. The reason for the decision to outsource, and for this vendor in particular, was cost and the firm's inexperience in developing web-based learning materials.

The management team set up two approaches to evaluation. One was to measure the outsourcing firm's products, that is, the degree to which they complied with standards, were on schedule, were instructionally sound, were compatible with current systems, the content was accurate, and learners accepted the courses. The second was for measuring the management team's effectiveness at providing oversight and direction, such as the degree to which the team follows the protocols, members feel their time is respected, and constituents think they are receiving adequate guidance and direction.

TOOL 7.4: GUIDELINES FOR MEASURING SUCCESS AND EFFECTIVENESS

This guideline is in two parts. Part 1 is designed to help the management team and outsourcing firm agree on a set of high-level measures. Part 2 is about what might be included in the outsourcing firm's annual performance review. Use only those parts and questions that are meaningful to you.

For Part 1, begin by revisiting the reason for outsourcing, because that was when the goals of the relationship should have been originally defined. The questions below are meant to help the team start the process.

Part 1: Success Measures

1. What are the key measures of performance indicators?

2. What criteria will we use to evaluate how effectively we are providing oversight?

   Did we meet our time commitments?

   Did we meet our budget commitments?

   Did we involve people the way we said we would?

   Did we behave in ways that supported dialogue, debate, and eventual consensus?

3. What criteria will we use to evaluate the effectiveness of our products and services?

   Test results?

   End-of-course evaluations?

   Correlate usage or participation with key business metrics, such as error rates, customer satisfaction, cost of sales, or pre-tax profits?

   Compliance with instructional standards and templates?

Part 2 is about the annual performance review. It addresses factors such as service level, cooperation, and celebrating success.

Annual Performance Review	Comments

Service Level: On what basis will you measure the outsourcing firm's service level? What factors will you consider?

- Conduct was courteous?
- Complied with security requirements as wore appropriate badges?
- The staffing level was agreed on?
- Hours of operation were agreed on?
- Personnel responded to complaints appropriately?
- Personnel followed the agreed-on protocols?

Annual Performance Review	**Comments**

- Reports were submitted on time?
- Reports were adequate to support decision making?
- Other?

Efficiency and Efficacy of the Outsourcing Firm's Operations: How and on what basis will you evaluate the outsourcing firm's efficiency? What factors will you consider?

- Agreed-on processes were followed?
- Identified processes requiring improvement were acted on?
- The amount of rework required?
- The need for additional resources?
- The number of resources required or actually used?
- The cost of the resources?
- Other?

Quality: On what basis will you evaluate the quality of the outsourcing firm's deliverables? What factors will you consider?

- Met standards?
- Learner acceptance?
- Content accuracy?
- Instructional materials and media functioned at the level expected?
- Test scores at the desired level?
- Learners' behavior changed on the job?
- Other?

Other Contract Terms:

- Used local resources?
- Used disadvantaged business enterprises?
- Used agreed-on software and systems?
- Performance bond and insurance were kept in force?
- Other?

CELEBRATE SUCCESS

The previous chapter dealt with dispute resolutions; however, equally important is how the group will recognize the accomplishments of team members and the group as a whole. There is a tendency to assume that finishing the work and getting paid are recognition enough; yet they are insufficient. When teams meet a deadline, introduce a time-saving or money-saving improvement, and successfully work though the elaborate political relationships that make up organizations, they should be recognized.

Celebrations are usually reserved for major deliverables or big project milestones. Unfortunately, waiting until the end of a project can be experienced as being very removed from the work that went into meeting the goal. Little celebrations, including personal recognition, such as a thank you or posting team and individual accomplishments on the website, can go a long way to assuring that people remain conscientious. A technique the management team might want to consider is to develop a list of ways to recognize people and their contributions. The list should include nonmonetary methods.

THE HR CONSULTING FIRM

The management team met to identify meaningful but inexpensive ways to recognize both members of the training function and employees of the outsourcing firm. Since the outsourcing firm's employees were from another country, the management team decided to list local attractions that might be of interest. They identified historic, amusement, entertainment, shopping, and recreation sites. Next, they identified mini-milestones on the project calendar that might be used to evaluate accomplishments of individuals and task forces.

The team also acquired books that contained discounts or free passes to movies and restaurants. It set up a page on the project's website to congratulate individuals and task forces for their work. They met with each of the task force teams when they were first commissioned to discuss appropriate tokens of recognition. The management team put recognition on its own calendar and held itself accountable for implementing the ideas the task forces suggested.

TOOL 7.5: GUIDELINES FOR RECOGNIZING ACCOMPLISHMENTS

This guideline is intended only to facilitate a discussion about who, how, and when to recognize individuals and task forces whose accomplishments are contributing to the success of the outsourcing relationship. The items listed below are just a beginning. It is important to remember that in the United States monetary recognition is considered taxable income and recipients should be told this in advance, as they may wonder why their $100 award was less. Also, you should ask someone from HR to suggest recognitions and rewards.

- Gift certificates to restaurants, movies, amusement parks, shopping, and so forth
- Catered team lunches
- Opportunities to meet senior managers
- Personal thank you notes
- Picture and bio on the website
- Letter in personnel file
- Underwriting attendance at a conference
- Financial awards

IMPROVE PROCESSES

The training function and the outsourcing firm's success depend on the efficiency and effectiveness of their processes. How work gets done consumes resources, including time, materials, systems, and money. If the way work gets done is inefficient, it is difficult to bring work in on time and within budget. Well-designed processes also facilitate working relationships because they help clarify roles and responsibilities. Here is a list of some of the typical processes required to design, develop, and deliver effective training:

- *Needs assessment*—the process used to discover and confirm stakeholder and organizational needs for learning solutions
- *Cause and job task analyses*—the process used to distinguish learning needs from other factors that may be impeding performance
- *Course design*—the process used to take the data from the job task analysis and convert it into a learning plan that includes curricula, courses, and modules
- *Course development*—the process used to convert the design into learning materials and into text and visuals
- *Materials production*—the process used to convert text and visuals into the chosen learning media
- *Administration*—the process used to register learners, track learning events, record test scores, and produce reports to support decisions
- *Implementation*—the process used to deploy learning solutions to the organization, including announcing their availability and facilitating participation

These processes should be documented to identify the steps, activities, and resources involved. The act of documenting should be one done in collaboration with the outsourcing firm so that all parties understand their roles and can challenge the necessity and sequence of activities. Documenting will identify redundant, missing, and non-value-adding steps. It will identify the resources used, including the subject-matter experts' time, design templates, and authoring systems, and provide an opportunity to identify missing, out-of-date, and inefficient resources. Tool 7.6 provides some guidelines for identifying the processes used by the outsourcing firm alone and in collaboration with the training function.

TOOL 7.6: GUIDELINES FOR
DOCUMENTING AND IMPROVING PROCESSES

Meet with representatives from the outsourcing firm and the training function. You can also do this with the management team or assign the task to a task force. Use the activities below to start:

1. Together list the processes used by the outsourcing firm and organization that will be required to satisfy the contract.

2. Identify the processes that are documented.

3. Identify the processes that should be documented and decide how to do this and who will do it.

4. Review the processes that are documented and discuss their viability in the organization's setting, their efficiency, and whether resources are used appropriately.

5. Identify the processes that should be improved by eliminating unnecessary steps, replacing out-of-date resources, or re-sequencing steps so work can be done in parallel or more efficiently.

6. Identify the measures or on what basis you will judge whether the processes improved.

7. Assign resources to document and prove those processes most needed to fulfill the contract.

IMPLICATIONS

The organization has the most to lose if the training function and outsourcing firm fail to deliver or provide the level of service expected; however, it might gain a better appreciation of how much training done poorly costs. The training function could use outsourcing as a way to improve its design and development processes, better track and control costs, and measure the effectiveness of the newly acquired capability or capacity, or it could use the relationship to rationalize its continued ineffectiveness. The success of the relationship depends on whether the training function embraces the opportunity to provide leadership or retreats under the guise it is a victim of senior management's myopic goal to cut costs.

MISSTEPS AND OVERSIGHTS

Here are some of the common oversights that can undermine the effectiveness of the outsourcing relationship. The training function takes the relationship with the outsourcing firm for granted and wants minimal involvement; it abdicates its leadership responsibility. The training function fails to leverage its intimate knowledge of the organization and provide the outsourcing firm with the intelligence required to work effectively with learners and management and get buy-in for its recommendations. The protocols and governance structure established during the transition are regarded as short-term transitory activities, not a long-term approach to sustaining a working relationship.

SUMMARY

The training function must decide what type of relationship it wants with the outsourcing firm. It can design one that builds trust and leads to a true partnership or it can walk away, abdicating any responsibility for governance and leadership. Both the training function and the outsourcing firm require leadership if they are to reap the benefits of sharing their capabilities. Leadership is what keeps the outsourcing firm and the training function focused on the needs of the organization. A public promise was made to the organization when the contract was signed, whether it was to reduce costs, deliver more rapidly, or expand the scope of training products and services. If the outsourcing firm fails to deliver on that promise, the training function need only look at its own inability to adequately provide direction and oversight. The training function and the outsourcing firm can develop standards and processes for learning products, record-keeping, and reports. Together they can develop protocols for interfacing with subject-matter experts, learners, other departments, and senior management that set new standards of excellence, or they can perpetuate the myth that training is a non-value-added but necessary expense.

**WHERE TO
LEARN MORE**

Here are some resources related to managing the training function:

Hale, J. (1995). *Standards for the training function.* Downers Grove, IL: Training Certification, Inc. Available at www.HaleAssociates.com.

International Board of Standards for Training, Performance, and Instruction. (2004). *Training manager competencies: The standards* (2nd ed.). Available at www.ibstpi.org.

Rosenbaum, S. *Learning paths: Increase profits by reducing the time it takes employees to get up-to-speed.* Available at www.learningpathconsultants.com or all online booksellers.

Phase 1: Identifying the Need	Phase 2: Assessing Capacity and Capability	Phase 3: Selecting the Outsourcing Firm	Phase 4: Contracting	Phase 5: Starting Up	Phase 6: Managing the Relationship	Phase 7: Closing Out
Determine client's needs	Assess strengths	Set the baseline	Prepare the contract	Build contract profile	Provide oversight	Notify about termination
a. shorten cycle times	a. credibility and trust	Define roles and responsibilities	Draft master agreement	Set up governance process	Implement the plan and protocols	Transfer intellectual property
b. deliver more training	b. capacity	Define the requirements	Determine scope of work	Develop management plan and schedule	Share expectations and agree on goals	Return physical property
• regulation	c. capability	Define the selection criteria	a. deliverables	Create communication protocols	Communicate	Reconcile financial obligations
• turnover	d. knowledge and skills	Recruit potential outsourcing firms	b. reporting requirements	Develop document standards and controls	Stay current with needs	Terminate clearances, codes
c. provide greater access to training	e. resources	Issue the RFQ	c. problem resolution	Agree on deliverable standards	Measure and report results	Execute final performance review
d. test learners' knowledge	f. work processes	Issue the RFP	d. quality and service level	Identify intellectual property	Celebrate success	Orient the training function
e. report on workforce capability	g. standards	Convene the panel and decide	e. timeliness and termination	Create transition plan	Improve processes	
f. expanding learning audience	Assess weaknesses		Draft addenda	Create dispute resolution process		
g. honor past and future commitments	Conduct job task analysis		Agree on terms and conditions			
Determine criticality and priority	a. by role		a. Accountability			
	b. by task and skill		b. Budget			
			c. Fees			
			d. Flexibility			
			e. Quality statement			
			f. Service level statement			

Figure 8.1. The Engagement Process, Phase 7: Closing Out

Chapter 8
Closing Out

*T*he chapter is about the last phase of The Engagement Process, during which the organization and outsourcing firm formally end their agreement (see Figure 8.1). Bringing an end to an agreement may sound contradictory to the intent of outsourcing, which is a long-term relationship. However, long-term relationships come to an end, even if they are to be renegotiated. Some agreements end because the work is done and the need satisfied. Others end because either the organization or the outsourcing firm wants to redefine the relationship or is unhappy with it. If the need for outsourcing services continues and the relationship is satisfactory, restarting the engagement process is still good business.

The organization should periodically reconfirm the scope of the need and ask its current outsourcing firm to reconfirm the competitiveness of its fees, the competency of its people, and the benefits of its technology.

The close-out can be relatively complicated, particularly if the relationship is complex. Even in simple, straightforward arrangements, certain things have to be reconciled for the relationship to be formally ended. It is similar to the transition plan, but in reverse. The transition plan was about enrolling the outsourcing firm, orienting it to the organization's culture, and bringing contract personnel up-to-speed on products, systems, course content, and the like. The close-out is the disengagement of the outsourcing firm's personnel and systems. Figure 8.2 is a high-level overview of the close-out process. It involves:

1. Notification of termination
2. Transfer of intellectual property
3. Return of physical property
4. Reconciliation of any financial obligations
5. Termination of security clearances, access codes, passes, and badges
6. Execution of the final performance review
7. Orientation of the training function in the use of the learning system and its technology.

149

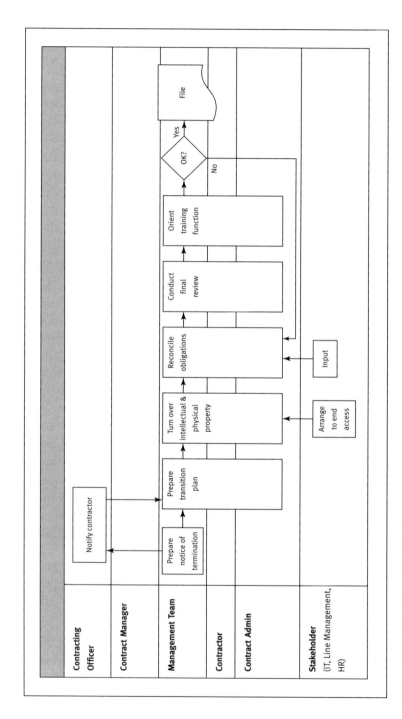

Figure 8.2. The Close-Out Process

NOTIFY ABOUT TERMINATION

This step is about giving notice to the outsourcing firm that the term of the contract is about to end and what the organization's intentions are, such as bring closure or reopen the solicitation process. How much notice to give depends on whether or not the time was stipulated in the contract and whether the relationship is to really end or to be renegotiated. If the relationship is to end, then the amount of notice could take months, depending on the complexity of the engagement and the anticipated time required to turn over the courseware and systems to the training function.

It is important to formally announce the intent, not assume the outsourcing firm knows. By announcing the intent to end the relationship, both parties can begin the process of disengagement.

TRANSFER INTELLECTUAL PROPERTY

The contract, either in the master agreement or addenda, should have specified what intellectual property was to be created by the outsourcing firm and who owned it. Intellectual property includes the courseware, learning objects, and data. For example, it includes all of the learning objects created or used in the development of the courseware, such as graphics, animation, video and audio clips, digital photographs, practice exercises, tests, job aids, logos, graphics, text, stories, and the like. Ideally, the management team arranged for all intellectual property to be identified, the source specified, and issues of ownership or rights resolved during the analysis and development processes.

If the learning objects were created by subcontractors, it is important to confirm who has title to the work. This information is essential if the training function wants to reuse the content without paying fees and if it wants the ability to modify the content using tools in the public domain. For example, if a photographer was hired to photograph people or equipment, someone should have a release of ownership rights to the work or a royalty agreement should have been signed. If the work was done using the outsourcing firm's proprietary software, the contract should have specified whether the organization would have licensing rights after the contract ended.

Ideally, the training function created a procedure for cataloging and tracking the inventory of courses, learner records, and learning objects at the beginning of the relationship. It should also have specified who was responsible for keeping track of all property, intellectual and physical, created, acquired, or licensed, during the term of the contract. Preferably, the outsourcing firm should not only provide an inventory of all items created, but also the source of the items and whether or not they were licensed. The transition is complete when the outsourcing firm turns over an inventory of the intellectual property noting its source and who owns it.

THE MANUFACTURER OF HEAVY EQUIPMENT

The manufacturer had built large, life-size cutaways of its equipment to use in the classroom. The cutaways represented a significant investment, as they included old and new equipment and advances in engineering technology.

The outsourcing firm used the cutaways to create photographs, computer-aided drawings, schematics, and the like to put into the computer-based and web-based curriculum. The training function listed the courseware as its intellectual property; however, it failed to list the individual graphics, renderings, and photographs that were embedded in the training. These individual objects constituted a sizeable investment that could be used in other training programs. The outsourcing firm agreed that the manufacturer owned them; however, this could have resulted in a costly dispute.

Tool 8.1 provides some guidelines to help you identify the intellectual property that should be transferred in title and physically to the training function.

TOOL 8.1: GUIDELINES FOR TRANSFERRING INTELLECTUAL PROPERTY

The management team should:

- Decide how to identify, label, and catalogue the intellectual property either created or acquired during the term of the contract.
- List all of the intellectual property. Be sure to include courseware and the learning objects that are embedded in them.
- If appropriate, distinguish between masters and copies.
- Note the medium.
- Note whether it was created or purchased.
- Note any restrictions such as whether licensing agreements are required and their terms.
- Define the process for turning the property over.
- Specify who on behalf of the training function is authorized to sign off that the transfer was complete.
- Set a date or time period.
- Execute the transfer.
- Prepare a document for the outsourcing firm noting that the transfer is complete.

RETURN PHYSICAL PROPERTY

During the course of the relationship, the outsourcing firm may have acquired or been given physical property to do the work. The property might include servers, software, laptops, tools, cutaways, and prototypes.[1] At the time, the training function may have assumed ownership, but not taken the time to catalogue the property. However, at the end of the contract, the property should be accounted for.

THE HR CONSULTING COMPANY

The company had contracted with an offshore outsourcing firm to develop approximately two hundred e-learning courseware modules to be delivered over the company's intranet. To allow call center personnel improved access to the courseware and to reduce the time it took for the company's IT department to deploy the courses to the intranet, an addendum was created to the original contract asking the outsourcing firm to acquire and host the e-learning content on a dedicated server located at the outsourcing firm's location. The hosted server also tracked records of what training call center personnel completed and their test scores. This data was sent nightly to the company's LMS, located at their headquarters. The addendum also specified that the outsourcing firm was to put in place a disaster recovery plan, should the host server fail, to protect the integrity of the data. The plan was to follow specifications provided by the company's IT department. As part of the disaster recovery plan, the outsourcing firm acquired a back-up server, located it in a different building, and stored back-ups of courseware and learner records, including test scores, course completion dates, and so forth.

The contract manager, in cooperation with the outsourcing firm's project manager, developed a protocol for listing, labeling, and cataloguing all intellectual and physical property used to carry out the contract. They also decided that, before the outsourcing firm could purchase any equipment or systems, a budget had to be submitted and approved. The company paid for all purchases and retained ownership of the physical property and the data. In this example, ownership of the real assets and of the data are also useful in addressing data privacy concerns that may occur when dealing with employees based around the world.

Tool 8.2 provides a set of guidelines for inventorying physical property acquired, given, or used by the outsourcing firm in the execution of their contract.

TOOL 8.2: GUIDELINES FOR TRANSFERRING PHYSICAL PROPERTY

The management team, and perhaps someone from Finance, should do the following:

1. Decide on how it is going to identify, label, and catalogue the physical property leased, allocated, or acquired during the term of the contract.

2. List all of the physical property.

3. Note the location of the property.

4. Define the process for turning the property over and be sure to include the authorization for movers and trucks if they are required.

5. Identify who should be involved, such as property management and finance.

6. Specify who on behalf of the training function is authorized to sign off that the transfer was complete.

7. Set a date or time period.

8. Execute the transfer.

9. Prepare a document for the outsourcing firm noting the transfer is complete.

Outsourcing Training and Development. Copyright © 2006 by John Wiley & Sons, Inc. Reproduced by permission of Pfeiffer, an Imprint of Wiley. www.pfeiffer.com

RECONCILE FINANCIAL OBLIGATIONS

In addition to intellectual and physical property, the training function and outsourcing firm should identify any debts or ongoing obligations, such as property leases, service contracts, royalties, and buyouts.[2] If property was allocated or leased, check the terms of the agreement to see whether there is any stipulation about who is responsible for improvements or restoring the space to the original state. If office equipment was acquired or allocated to the outsourcing firm, find out whether there are any service agreements or stipulations requiring either an ongoing or periodic payment. If royalty agreements were signed, find out the terms.

During the course of the contract, the outsourcing firm may have entered into contracts such as service agreements or invested in improvements to work space. If ownership of the equipment and space will be assumed by the training function, the financial obligations may be transferred as well. For example, the outsourcing firm may have been assigned property owned by the organization. While using the property, the outsourcing firm may have made improvements to the property so it better met its needs, such as put in cubicles, added electrical circuits, and added cabling for increased Internet connections. The question to be answered is: "Who, if anyone, is financially obligated once the contract with the outsourcing firm has ended?"

THE HR CONSULTING COMPANY

The company's facilities management department located space for the fifty specialists who worked for the outsourcing firm. The space had to be physically near IT and the training function to facilitate coordination between the groups. However, before the space could be truly functional, additional cabling had to be installed to allow for access to the company's intranet and the Internet. The specialists also required desks, chairs, phones, and other traditional office equipment. The outsourcing firm's specialists brought their own laptop computers, but asked for access to printers, faxes, and copy machines. At the time of the close-out, finance identified property, assets, and obligations that had been overlooked, such as the lease for the space where the back-up server was located.

Some guidelines to help you identify any hidden financial obligations are shown in Tool 8.3.

TOOL 8.3: GUIDELINES FOR RECONCILING FINANCIAL OBLIGATIONS

The management team, and perhaps someone from the property management, maintenance, or finance departments, should do the following:

1. Identify any leased space used by the outsourcing firm and determine who is liable for the lease and the provisions for terminating it.

2. Identify any space owned or leased by the organization but used by the outsourcing firm and review the procedure for vacating the space. Be sure to determine whether the training function or the outsourcing firm has any liabilities for vacating or restoring the space.

3. Identify any service agreements and determine when they end, whether they are still of value, and find out whether and how they can be transferred to the organization if they are in the name of the outsourcing firm.

4. Determine whether any buyouts are required and what the terms are.

5. Define the process for reconciling the obligations.

6. Specify who on behalf of the training function is authorized to sign off that the obligations are reconciled or satisfied.

7. Set a date or time period by which the reconciliation is to be complete.

8. Prepare a document for the outsourcing firm noting that the reconciliation is complete.

TERMINATE CLEARANCES, CODES

At or near the beginning and over the course of the contract, the outsourcing firm's people were given access codes, identification badges, and parking passes. The training function should have arranged for a complete listing of the people who were authorized to have access to data, systems, and property. Someone should have maintained a list of people who were given identification badges, parking passes, and the like. Perhaps the passes, access codes, and badges are time-sensitive and self-destruct within a given time period. If not, they should be turned in. At the same time, the IT department should reset or nullify all pass codes and communication links.

Since the close-out is usually not executed on one single day but over a period of time, the management team should set up a phase-out plan whereby access to property, data, and internal websites ends when the work ends. An important part of this step is notifying the organization that access is being stopped so learners and managers do not continue to request work from the outsourcing firm's people.

Tool 8.4 contains some guidelines to help you identify any passes, badges, or other provisions that give people access to the organization's facilities or data.

TOOL 8.4: GUIDELINES FOR TERMINATING SECURITY CLEARANCES

The management team, and perhaps someone from risk management and IT, should:

1. Identify the people who were given pass codes, clearances, passes, and the like.

2. Create a calendar noting when people's access to property, data, databases, internal websites, and the like will end, perhaps based on the finalization of any deliverables or completion of specific assignments.

3. Develop a procedure for turning in all passes and canceling access.

4. Notify the outsourcing firm's people when and how they are expected to turn in any passes.

5. Set up a schedule to nullify pass codes.

6. Specify who on behalf of the training function is authorized to confirm the termination of security clearances.

7. Set a date or time period by which all security clearances are to end.

8. Monitor that the termination is being done as planned and on schedule.

EXECUTE FINAL PERFORMANCE REVIEW

It would be easy and perhaps more comfortable to end an engagement without conducting a formal review; however, the review is an opportunity for both sides to reflect, discuss, and exchange what they gained from the relationship. At a minimum, each side should privately review its expectations, disappointments, and delights. Each should identify what was gained that it wants to apply or avoid in future engagements.

The purpose of the formal review is to officially document in a summary form what the organization gained from the relationship and what the outsourcing firm might do differently or do the same next time. The review is when the training function's and outsourcing firm's contract managers meet to go over the items they identified that they wanted to review on an annual basis, such as goal accomplishment, service level, cooperation, cost savings, and so forth. (See Tool 8.5, Guidelines for the Final Performance Review.) Both sides should have gained from the relationship. Hopefully, what was gained was significantly more than what was spelled out in the contract. Both sides should be able to identify areas in which they were prepared or unprepared to carry out their side of the agreement.

TOOL 8.5: GUIDELINES FOR THE FINAL PERFORMANCE REVIEW

These guidelines are in two parts. Part 1 is intended for the training function and outsourcing firm to do independently. Part 2 is for the training function and outsourcing firm to do in collaboration.

Part 1. To Be Completed Separately

Meet with representatives from the training function. The outsourcing firm should do the same with its people who were assigned to your contract. The training function can use and modify the questions below to prepare for its meeting with representatives of the outsourcing firm.

1. How effective were we at providing oversight?
2. How well did we model using the communication protocols that were mutually established?
3. How well did we execute our responsibility to provide feedback?
4. How well did we execute our responsibility to assure the integrity of the goods and services developed or provided by the outsourcing firm?
5. How well did we assure that intellectual property was identified and issues of ownership satisfactorily resolved?

6. How well did we carry out our responsibility to act as stewards of the organization's resources and assets?

7. Did we achieve the goals that outsourcing was expected to accomplish?

8. What can we do differently, in a more timely fashion, more consistently, or more thoroughly to assure that future outsourcing relationships better fulfill the goals of the engagement?

Use your answers to develop an action plan for the team should you enter into a relationship with the same or a different outsourcing firm in the future.

Part 2. To Be Completed Together

Refer to the performance review form suggested in Chapter 7, Tool 7.4, Part 2. If you want to add any items to the list, the outsourcing firm should have been notified in advance.

1. Ask the outsourcing firm to rate itself on the items in the review form.

2. Ask the training team to rate the outsourcing firm on the items in the review form.

3. Ask the training team to discuss and agree on what it wants as an outcome from doing the final review. Remember that, since this is the final review, the exchange should be constructive for both the training team and the outsourcing firm, not cathartic.

4. Identify areas in which you think feedback would be helpful.

5. Arrange a time to meet that is mutually beneficial.

6. Assuming the intent is for the exchange to be helpful, ask the outsourcing firm to share its insights after having completed the review form.

7. Summarize the training team's insights from having completed the review form, both about its own behavior and that of the outsourcing team members.

ORIENT THE TRAINING FUNCTION

Finally, the training function needs to understand and be able to use the courseware developed by the outsourcing firm. The training function's role may have been minor in the development of the courseware; however, to reap the benefits, it must be able to manage and administer the deliverables created by the outsourcing firm. It might be helpful to assume that the responsibility for training and development will revert to the training function, requiring it to be more capable perhaps than it was at the beginning of the engagement. Tool 8.6 provides guidelines on orienting the training function.

TOOL 8.6: GUIDELINES FOR ORIENTING THE TRAINING FUNCTION

The management team should decide what it wants to accomplish as a result of the orientation. It should describe the outcomes in as much detail as possible. Given that the goal is for the training function to more effectively manage training, ask the following questions:

- What do members of the training function want to better understand about what the outsourcing firm did and why?
- What do members of the training function want to better understand about the products developed by the outsourcing firm or services rendered?
- What can the outsourcing firm do or explain that would be of value to the training function?
- What does the outsourcing firm recommend the training function to do or do differently and why?

IMPLICATIONS

The transfer of intellectual and physical property to the training function requires the function to put in place processes and procedures for managing its portfolio of products. It must assume responsibility for maintaining the deliverables and assuring they are relevant. During the engagement, the training function had an opportunity to improve its capabilities and capacity. It had the opportunity to assure that its products and services were aligned with the organization's needs and added value. Once the engagement ends, the training function has an opportunity to be a full performance partner with its internal clients.

MISSTEPS

Some of the missteps that training functions make is that they fail to fully leverage the capabilities of the outsourcing firm by not increasing their own capabilities. They under-appreciate the need for excellent vendor and project management skills. They fail to apply the communication protocols with their clients. They undervalue the importance of clarifying the deliverables and ownership of the intellectual properties produced as a result of the engagement.

SUMMARY

Outsourcing can be an opportunity to reenergize the training function by helping it assure its products and services are focused on the organization's goals and putting in place products and processes that are effective. The end of a contract can be a time of celebration or of remorse, depending on the relationship. It is important to formally recognize the end, take responsibility for reconciling the work performed, and identify what was learned from the relationship.

WHERE TO LEARN MORE

Outsourcing is a business model that should be based on a well-thought-out strategic plan. Here is a book that is specific to strategic planning for the training function. It may be old, but it is very good. It is available through www.amazon.com.

Svenson, R., & Rinderer, M. (1992). *The training and development strategic plan workbook.* Upper Saddle River, NJ: Prentice Hall.

NOTES

1. A cutaway is a section of a piece of equipment or object so the internal workings can be seen. Examples include models of hearts made out of plastic, showing the valves and veins, and sections of engines, showing the mechanical components. They are used to demonstrate the internal workings of equipment, parts, and systems.
2. A buyout is an agreement to buy an asset either at fair market value or by paying off any outstanding debt. The outsourcing firm may want the right to buy assets acquired by the organization so it could do the work. Similarly, the organization may want the right to buy assets acquired or created by the outsourcing firm.

Index

About the Author

Judith Hale, CPT, has dedicated her career to helping management professionals develop effective, practical ways to improve individual and organizational performance. She has used the techniques, processes, and job aids described in this book in her own consulting work, which has spanned twenty-five years. Judith's clients speak of the practicality of her approach and the proven results it yields. She is able to explain complex ideas so that people understand their relevance and can apply them to their own situations. She is able to help others come to a shared understanding about what to do and how to commit to action.

Her consulting firm, Hale Associates, was founded in 1974 and enjoys long-term relationships with a variety of major corporations. The services her firm provides include consultation on alignment, assessment, certification, evaluation, integration of performance improvement systems, performance management, and strategic planning.

She is the author of *The Performance Consultant's Fieldbook, Performance-Based Evaluation,* and *Performance-Based Certification.* Her book *Achieving a Leadership Role for Training* describes how training can apply the standards espoused by the International Standards Organization and Baldrige to its own operation. She was the topic editor for *Designing Work Groups, Jobs, and Work Flow* and for *Designing Cross-Functional Business Processes* and the author of the chapter "The Hierarchy of Interventions" in the *Sourcebook for Performance Improvement.* Judith also wrote *The Training Manager Competencies: The Standards,* as well as *The Training Function Standards* and *Standards for Qualifying Trainers,* and she put together the *Workbook and Job Aids*

171

for Good Fair Tests, and was a contributor to *What Smart Trainers Know,* edited by Lorraine Ukens (2001, Jossey-Bass/Pfeiffer).

Judith is an appointed member of the Illinois Occupational Skills Standard and Credentialing Council. She is a past president of the International Society for Performance Improvement (ISPI). NSPI named her Outstanding Member of the Year in 1987. She has also served as president of the International Board of Standards for Performance and Instruction and president of the Chicago chapter of the Industrial Relations Research Association (IRRA). She was a commercial arbitrator with the American Arbitration Association and has been a member of the American Society for Training and Development (ASTD) for many years. She was nominated for ASTD's Gordon Bliss Award in 1995. She taught graduate courses in management for fourteen years for the Insurance School of Chicago and received the school's Outstanding Educator award in 1986.

Judith speaks regularly at ASTD International, ASTD Technical Skills, the International Society for Performance Improvement, and VNU Learning's 's annual training conferences.

Judith holds a B.A. from Ohio State University (communication), an M.A. from Miami University (theater management), and a Ph.D. from Purdue University (instructional design, with minors in organizational communication and adult education). She has received the International Society for Performance Improvement's certification, Certified Performance Technologist.

Pfeiffer Publications Guide

This guide is designed to familiarize you with the various types of Pfeiffer publications. The formats section describes the various types of products that we publish; the methodologies section describes the many different ways that content might be provided within a product. We also provide a list of the topic areas in which we publish.

FORMATS

In addition to its extensive book-publishing program, Pfeiffer offers content in an array of formats, from fieldbooks for the practitioner to complete, ready-to-use training packages that support group learning.

FIELDBOOK Designed to provide information and guidance to practitioners in the midst of action. Most fieldbooks are companions to another, sometimes earlier, work, from which its ideas are derived; the fieldbook makes practical what was theoretical in the original text. Fieldbooks can certainly be read from cover to cover. More likely, though, you'll find yourself bouncing around following a particular theme, or dipping in as the mood, and the situation, dictate.

HANDBOOK A contributed volume of work on a single topic, comprising an eclectic mix of ideas, case studies, and best practices sourced by practitioners and experts in the field.

An editor or team of editors usually is appointed to seek out contributors and to evaluate content for relevance to the topic. Think of a handbook not as a ready-to-eat meal, but as a cookbook of ingredients that enables you to create the most fitting experience for the occasion.

RESOURCE Materials designed to support group learning. They come in many forms: a complete, ready-to-use exercise (such as a game); a comprehensive resource on one topic (such as conflict management) containing a variety of methods and approaches; or a collection of like-minded activities (such as icebreakers) on multiple subjects and situations.

TRAINING PACKAGE An entire, ready-to-use learning program that focuses on a particular topic or skill. All packages comprise a guide for the facilitator/trainer and a workbook for the participants. Some packages are supported with additional media—such as video—or learning aids, instruments, or other devices to help participants understand concepts or practice and develop skills.

- *Facilitator/trainer's guide* Contains an introduction to the program, advice on how to organize and facilitate the learning event, and step-by-step instructor notes. The guide also contains copies of presentation materials—handouts, presentations, and overhead designs, for example—used in the program.

- *Participant's workbook* Contains exercises and reading materials that support the learning goal and serves as a valuable reference and support guide for participants in the weeks and months that follow the learning event. Typically, each participant will require his or her own workbook.

ELECTRONIC CD-ROMs and web-based products transform static Pfeiffer content into dynamic, interactive experiences. Designed to take advantage of the searchability, automation, and ease-of-use that technology provides, our e-products bring convenience and immediate accessibility to your workspace.

METHODOLOGIES

CASE STUDY A presentation, in narrative form, of an actual event that has occurred inside an organization. Case studies are not prescriptive, nor are they used to prove a point; they are designed to develop critical analysis and decision-making skills. A case study has a specific time frame, specifies a sequence of events, is narrative in structure, and contains a plot structure—an issue (what should be/have been done?). Use case studies when the goal is to enable participants to apply previously learned theories to the circumstances in the case, decide what is pertinent, identify the real issues, decide what should have been done, and develop a plan of action.

ENERGIZER A short activity that develops readiness for the next session or learning event. Energizers are most commonly used after a break or lunch to stimulate or refocus the group. Many involve some form of physical activity, so they are a useful way to counter post-lunch lethargy. Other uses include transitioning from one topic to another, where "mental" distancing is important.

EXPERIENTIAL LEARNING ACTIVITY (ELA) A facilitator-led intervention that moves participants through the learning cycle from experience to application (also known as a Structured Experience). ELAs are carefully thought-out designs in which there is a definite learning purpose and intended outcome. Each step—everything that participants do during the activity—facilitates the accomplishment of the stated goal. Each ELA includes complete instructions for facilitating the intervention and a clear statement of goals, suggested group size and timing, materials required, an explanation of the process, and, where appropriate, possible variations to the activity. (For more detail on Experiential Learning Activities, see the Introduction to the *Reference Guide to Handbooks and Annuals*, 1999 edition, Pfeiffer, San Francisco.)

GAME A group activity that has the purpose of fostering team spirit and togetherness in addition to the achievement of a pre-stated goal. Usually contrived—undertaking a desert expedition, for example—this type of learning method offers an engaging means for participants to demonstrate and practice business and interpersonal skills. Games are effective for team building and personal development mainly because the goal is subordinate to the process—the means through which participants reach decisions, collaborate, communicate, and generate trust and understanding. Games often engage teams in "friendly" competition.

ICEBREAKER A (usually) short activity designed to help participants overcome initial anxiety in a training session and/or to acquaint the participants with one another. An icebreaker can be a fun activity or can be tied to specific topics or training goals. While a useful tool in itself, the icebreaker comes into its own in situations where tension or resistance exists within a group.

INSTRUMENT A device used to assess, appraise, evaluate, describe, classify, and summarize various aspects of human behavior. The term used to describe an instrument depends primarily on its format and purpose. These terms include survey, questionnaire, inventory, diagnostic, survey, and poll. Some uses of instruments include providing instrumental feedback to group members, studying here-and-now processes or functioning within a group, manipulating group composition, and evaluating outcomes of training and other interventions.

Instruments are popular in the training and HR field because, in general, more growth can occur if an individual is provided with a method for focusing specifically on his or her own behavior. Instruments also are used to obtain information that will serve as a basis for change and to assist in workforce planning efforts.

Paper-and-pencil tests still dominate the instrument landscape with a typical package comprising a facilitator's guide, which offers advice on administering the instrument and interpreting the collected data, and an initial set of instruments. Additional instruments are available separately. Pfeiffer, though, is investing heavily in e-instruments. Electronic instrumentation provides effortless distribution and, for larger groups particularly, offers advantages over paper-and-pencil tests in the time it takes to analyze data and provide feedback.

LECTURETTE A short talk that provides an explanation of a principle, model, or process that is pertinent to the participants' current learning needs. A lecturette is intended to establish a common language bond between the trainer and the participants by providing a mutual frame of reference. Use a lecturette as an introduction to a group activity or event, as an interjection during an event, or as a handout.

MODEL A graphic depiction of a system or process and the relationship among its elements. Models provide a frame of reference and something more tangible, and more easily remembered, than a verbal explanation. They also give participants something to "go on," enabling them to track their own progress as they experience the dynamics, processes, and relationships being depicted in the model.

ROLE PLAY A technique in which people assume a role in a situation/scenario: a customer service rep in an angry-customer exchange, for example. The way in which the role is approached is then discussed and feedback is offered. The role play is often repeated using a different approach and/or incorporating changes made based on feedback received. In other words, role playing is a spontaneous interaction involving realistic behavior under artificial (and safe) conditions.

SIMULATION A methodology for understanding the interrelationships among components of a system or process. Simulations differ from games in that they test or use a model that depicts or mirrors some aspect of reality in form, if not necessarily in content. Learning occurs by studying the effects of change on one or more factors of the model. Simulations are commonly used to test hypotheses about what happens in a system—often referred to as "what if?" analysis—or to examine best-case/worst-case scenarios.

THEORY A presentation of an idea from a conjectural perspective. Theories are useful because they encourage us to examine behavior and phenomena through a different lens.

TOPICS

The twin goals of providing effective and practical solutions for workforce training and organization development and meeting the educational needs of training and human resource professionals shape Pfeiffer's publishing program. Core topics include the following:

Leadership & Management

Communication & Presentation

Coaching & Mentoring

Training & Development

E-Learning

Teams & Collaboration

OD & Strategic Planning

Human Resources

Consulting